RELIEF PRINTMAKING

GERALD F. BROMMER

RELIEF PRINTMAKING

Contemporary printmakers might well envy the craftsmanship of the common bark beetle. This print was pulled from the inked side of a log from which the bark had been removed. Notice the variation in details—you can also see the repetition of other patterns.

DAVIS PUBLICATIONS, INC.
WORCESTER, MASSACHUSETTS

The Horses. *Don la Viere Turner, woodcut, (48 x 84). Probably the largest print shown in this book, it took nearly all of a 4 x 8 foot sheet of plywood to complete. Many motor driven tools were employed in working on this huge surface. Collection, Pasadena Art Museum, California.*

Copyright 1970

Davis Publications, Inc.
Worcester, Massachusetts, U.S.A.

Library of Congress Catalog Card Number: 77-113860
SBN 87192-034-4

Graphic Design by the Author
Consulting Editors: George F. Horn
             Sarita R. Rainey

CONTENTS

To Georgia

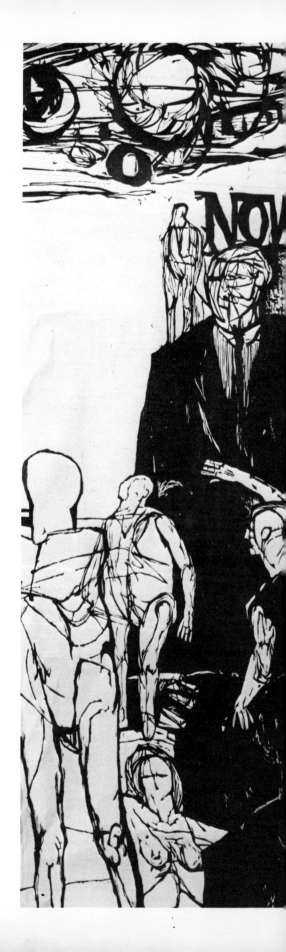

FOREWORD

Throughout history, the art of man has gone through an orderly process of change — in purpose, in content, in style and in materials used in the shaping of various forms of visual imagery. Prior to the latter part of the 19th Century, art was more or less regional or national and persistently traditional in nature.

In contrast, during the 20th Century, particularly the latter half, the work of the artist has been characterized by dynamic change — accelerated change — extreme change. Movements and directions have occurred in rapid succession, each replacing the other in a relatively short span of time. Today's artist has presented us with a whole new visual language — abstract symbols, kinetics, sound, light, environment. Inventions, discoveries, science and technology — new materials, techniques and tools — have all been forces in the spontaneous and individualistic quest of the 20th Century artist. But the dominant force, without doubt, has been the spirit of the artist in a mobile society — searching, exploring, innovating.

It is this spirit that Jerry Brommer projects so well as a teacher, artist, author. This new book brings to students and teachers alike, an exciting and challenging adventure in printmaking. Each page is a new experience, an inspiration and an imaginative 20th Century approach to an ancient art form. Journey through the book and a whole new world of creative printmaking will open up for you.

— George F. Horn

Limited Perspective. *Richard Wiegmann produced this woodcut which features numerous textural treatments contrasted with strong solid shapes. It is 23 x 33¹/₄ in size.*

BEFORE BEGINNING

Stimulation is what is offered in this book. Ideas and suggestions are proposed for any of several dozen ways of working with the relief surface, but there are too many projects for any teacher or individual to handle in one or two semesters of printmaking. So the book is really an idea file, replete with how-to-do-it techniques, suggestions for expansion of working methods, fundamental and traditional approaches, wild and far-out adaptations, and always encouragement to try—to delve a bit further into the realm of relief printmaking.

Much time and space are spent on the basic and fundamental linoleum cut and woodcut, because I feel the need for this background before experimental printmaking is attempted. The newer and possibly more exciting variations of the relief print are dealt with in varying degrees of completeness. Using the fundamental approaches as background, the more experimental work can proceed in individual directions.

The book can be used to provide teachers with ready reference material. It should help instructors understand the problems and assist in solving them. The multitude of pictures and prints should suggest assignments and inspire alternatives, since none is spelled out with much detail in the body of the book.

The large section on experimental prints can be used selectively as a source of assignments for the class, or can be used as a reference tool, suggesting many directions but allowing for individual choice of problems. (See chapter 9, the section on "Problems and Assignments" and "Sources for Ideas".) The book is a fine source for materials and methods and should inspire more confident and enthusiastic teaching.

Students should find in this book the stimulus to experiment and achieve. The hundreds of photos of work should inspire, suggest or lead into new ways of thinking and working. Some of the work illustrated cannot be accomplished by students in classroom situations; indeed some are not even relief prints. But they are included to stimulate thinking and provide avenues of direction. Look at them carefully.

Young printmakers should realize that there is no end to the techniques—the ones in this book can suggest newer innovations which, in turn, can lead to others in chain-reaction fashion. They can find here all the information needed to produce excellent traditional prints (which they should try) as well as contemporary expressions through the use of built-up surfaces and experimental printing techniques (which they should also try).

Don't overlook the sections in each chapter called "Other Ideas", because many exciting techniques, variations and ideas are crammed into a little space there.

The way subject matter and methods of working are increasing in scope, there is literally no end in sight. A printmaking medium that began as only a woodcut centuries ago is today clothed in the contemporary garb of innovation and experimentation. Let this book open new doors for you.

Begin . . .   G. F. B.

1

LA FLUTE

FV

2

3

8

INTRODUCING THE RELIEF PRINT

The first art activity that a child engages in, although not consciously, is that of relief printing. The nurse applies a bit of ink to the sole of the baby's feet, the doctor presses them against paper . . . and a print is made. The youngster proceeds to produce all kinds of prints: jelly print on cupboard, mud print on wall, and cereal print on high chair. He witnesses other prints also: automobile tire in mud, wet footprint on floor, and Mom's lipstick kiss print on his own forehead.

The fascination with materials that can be used for reproducing forms sticks with students all through school, and actually the anticipation and surprise of seeing a print pulled from the inked surface is ever new. Children are intrigued with the ability of a potato or carrot to print, and the intrigue seems to stimulate them to greater production.

Young people have an insatiable desire to manipulate tools and work with various materials in new and different ways. And they need this exposure to exciting new things to make them more perceptive, aware and thinking students, because, in the process, they are on their way to becoming more complete individuals. The materials, tools, and methods of working with relief printmaking are vehicles toward perceptive development. And it is toward stimulating perceptive development that this book addresses itself. It should provide not only many hours of fascinating work and dozens of ideas, but it should aid in the full development of the art student, exposing him to new and varied modes of communication.

Before delving into the many facets of the relief print technique, we should see where it all began, how it fits into the total print-

1 The art room is a place to experiment and experience . . . both are taking place in this printmaking class.
2 The Flute. *Felix Vallotton. Plate II from the suite "Six Instruments de Musique." A simple and bold woodcut. Collection, Museum of Modern Art, New York. Gift of Victor S. Riesenfeld.*
3 Lyric of Kyoto. *Rikio Takahashi, woodcut, (36 x 24). A large woodcut, done in many colors that overlap each other, producing still more colors. Notice that some areas are textured while others are not. Courtesy, M. M. Shinno.*

1

2

making picture, just what relief printing is, and where it is all going. Let's take a brief look.

A LOOK BACK

Representation and communication through visual symbols has been one of man's continual needs since the beginning of time. Artists have fulfilled the function as creators of these images, producing sculpture, paintings, frescoes, carvings, and various other forms of art to carry the message.

The need for a broader form of communication than the single original painting could produce was the impetus which spawned the art of printmaking. The origin of relief printing is lost in antiquity, but first the Egyptians, then the Chinese and Japanese used hand-carved relief designs that could be reproduced in numbers. Textile designs were hand printed from relief blocks in Western Europe in medieval times, and by the 13th century woodcut relief prints were commonplace for printing greeting cards, playing cards, and calendars.

Other forms of producing multiple-original works of art followed; the etching and engraving, the lithograph and the serigraph. But printmakers today who work in relief print media are partaking of both the oldest and newest techniques . . . revitalized graphic reproductive techniques that know no limits. (See chapter 9, the section on "Historical Information", for names of many historically important printmakers.)

The first extant pictorial woodcuts date from the end of the 14th century and probably came from Germany, while in France and Holland woodcuts were also produced at an early date. Two factors influenced the spread of woodcuts in the 14th century; one was the introduction of paper into Europe; the other was the growing practice of having private prayers, which created a demand for inexpensive substitutes for costly paintings in the churches. This is why the earliest woodcuts were fairly large single sheets with representations of religious subjects.

At first these prints were line drawings that were colored by hand, but later they were replaced by modeled figures created by intricate crosshatching to show shadows. At this stage, the result was really alien to the technique, since printmakers were trying to make prints appear as ink drawings.

1 Madonna and Child. *This 7 x 5 wood engraving was done by Timothy Cole, and illustrates the traditional use made of the engraving techniques. Collection, Pasadena Art Museum, California. Bequest of Josephine P. Everett.*
2 Corral. *Lew Ott, wood engraving, (4 x 10). Using the same tools as craftsmen have handled for centuries, the contemporary artist works his blocks to satisfy his current form of communication. Courtesy, Orlando Gallery, Encino, California.*
3 The Holy Trinity. *Albrecht Dürer, woodcut, (15¹/₂ x 11¹/₄). Intricate detail, that would be difficult to reproduce in pen and ink, characterize the work of one of the world's greatest printmakers. Collection, Los Angeles County Museum of Art. Gift of the Dan Murphy Foundation.*

3

近江八景之内

唐崎夜雨

祇の松の
のよ聲
まく代
にく夜
うら雨
るのの

廣重画

1

1 Night Rain on Karasaki Pine. *This woodblock print by Utagawa Hiroshige is from the 8 views of Omi series and is 8⁷/₈ x 13⁷/₈. Collection, Los Angeles County Museum of Art. Gift of Mr. and Mrs. Nathan V. Hammer.*
2 Shell Horn. *R. Mizufune, contemporary Japanese woodcut, (30 x 18). Thick ink in more than ten colors was used in this print, which has a printed surface resembling that of an impasto painting. Courtesy, M. M. Shinno.*
3 The Great Wave at Satta, Shunshu. *Hiroshige's print is from the 36 views of Fuji series. This traditional Japanese multi-colored woodcut is 13¹/₂ x 8¹/₂. Collection, Pasadena Art Museum, California. Estate of Mrs. James W. Johnson.*
4 Morning C. *Rikio Takahashi, color woodcut, (24 x 20). Many colors and many shapes are combined in this exciting design. Once the registration problems are solved, such printing can be accomplished with relative ease. Courtesy, M. M. Shinno.*

2

Michael Wohlgemut, in 1460, began to work the block in a way that produced fine prints, and Germany led in this technique until its peak in Albrecht Dürer's day, nearly a century later.

When the Renaissance demanded finer lines and more elaborate detail, metal line engraving replaced the woodcut, and the relief print was used primarily for illustration. It was revived as a fine art medium in the 19th century and by the end of that century was the idiom of the Expressionist Movement. Meanwhile, photography replaced it as an illustration technique, and that is where we stood some twenty years ago.

The Japanese colored woodcut, as we have come to know it from the beautiful prints in our museums, was developed in the 1760s and reached its peak by the end of the 18th century. They had used simple black and white linecuts from the eighth century until then.

The drastic change in technique was brought about by Moronobu, who lived in the latter half of the 17th century, and his multi-colored woodcuts offered the masses a substitute for expensive paintings. The 18th century resurgence was led by Haronobu who made the multicolor print an independent art form, no longer merely a method for reproducing old paintings. This method involved printing 20 or more different blocks to produce 20 or more colors in the print. The artist designed and drew the blocks, a cutter did all the work of removing unwanted wood, and a master printer pulled all the prints. It was a masterful job of cooperation and coordination. This complicated and precise method of working was a perfect medium for transposing the Japanese concept of life into an art form. The color woodcuts of Hokusai had a profound influence on many late 19th century European artists, and through them have affected the direction of 20th century art.

Printing principles in the 20th century are virtually the same today as they were hundreds of years ago. However, the era of experimentation has brought with it hundreds of new applications and adaptations in the techniques for making original relief prints. That is one of the purposes of this book, to make you and your students aware of them, and to put these new techniques at your disposal. As in other phases of art, this is where the excitement of the 20th century is evident—in experimentation and the use of new materials and techniques.

MAJOR PRINTMAKING TECHNIQUES

The terms "print" and "printmaking" apply to all forms of producing multiple-original works, even though each medium has its own particular appearance. The best way to differentiate between prints is based on the method by which they were produced: planographic, relief, intaglio and stencil. The name used for each of these approaches is lithography, woodcut, etching and engraving, and serigraphy or silk-screen printing. Let's look a bit at each technique and see how they differ.

3

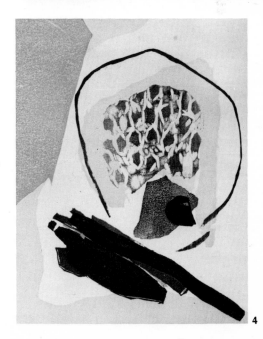

4

THE PLANOGRAPHIC PROCESS — LITHOGRAPHY

A lithographic drawing is made on a block of smooth limestone with a grease pencil. There is nothing difficult about this process, but the drawing must leave grease on the stone. After chemical treatment with nitric acid and gum arabic which etches and cleans the stone, water is sponged over the surface. A large ink-charged leather roller is passed over wet limestone and ink is accepted by the greased areas. A dampened sheet of paper is placed on the inked stone, which sits on the bed of a lithographic press, and stone, ink and paper undergo the scraping pressure of the press as they pass beneath a heavy blade.

The process is essentially a chemical one, being based on the antipathy between water and grease. It is a *surface* phenomenon (planographic), since the image on the stone is neither above nor below the surface being printed.

1 Hermine Korner. *Oskar Kokoschka produced this 26¹/₂ x 19¹/₂ lithograph in blue ink. Collection, Los Angeles County Museum of Art. Gift of the Graphic Arts Council Fund.*
2 White Line Square. *Josef Albers produced a series of lithographs in 1966 that featured such squares. This print, number VIII in the Series, is 20³/₄ x 20³/₄. Collection, Los Angeles County Museum of Art. Gift of Gemini, Ltd., the studio in which Albers worked.*
3 The White Calf. *This 10 x 12³/₄ lithograph was done by Thomas Hart Benton and is in the collection of the Pasadena Art Museum, California. Gift of Jerome A. Schiell.*
4 Untitled. *Claes Oldenburg has produced a series of lithographs that were done from his notes in 1968; the prints make use of almost every available lithographic technique. Printed in several colors, this print is done by lithography, even the parts that look like ruled paper and masking tape. The print is 22¹/₂ x 15¹/₂. Collection, Los Angeles County Museum of Art. Lent by Mr. and Mrs. David Gensburg.*
5 *Numerous textures are available on the grainy surface of the lithographic stone. Most range from brush strokes of tusche to charcoal-like shading of the lithographic crayon. Detail from Cows by Arthur Geisert. Collection of the author.*

2

3

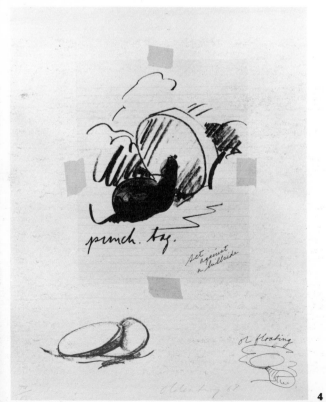

4

5

1

2

3

DIE LEBENDEN DEM TOTEN . ERINNERUNG AN DEN 15.JANUAR 1919

THE RELIEF PROCESS — WOODCUT

With a well-sharpened knife, the printmaker cuts and gouges a piece of plank wood, removing all areas which he wants to remain white on his print. These are cut from the drawing which the artist penciled on the block. The raised part of wood remaining at the level of the original surface is the part that will receive ink from a loaded brayer. When paper is placed on the inked block and pressure is applied, either by burnishing or by placing in a press, the ink is transferred to paper—producing the print known as a woodcut. The image to be printed stands in *relief* on the block of wood.

1 Boat. *Lew Ott, wood engraving, (4 x 6). Small sized blocks and intricate detail and pattern are characteristics of this medium. Courtesy, Orlando Gallery, Encino, California.*
2 The Clouds. *David Glines produced this 12 x 9 wood engraving composed of delicately cut lines contrasted with bold dark shapes. Collection, Pasadena Art Museum, California.*
3 Weighing Fish. *Antonio Frasconi, color woodcut, (10¹/₂ x 7³/₄). The directness and strength of the composition make it appear to be larger than it really is. Collection, Pasadena Art Museum, California. Gift of Weyhe Gallery.*
4 Funeral of Rosa Luxembourg. *Käthe Kollwitz, woodcut, (15⁷/₈ x 21¹/₈). The same strength that appears in the artist's lithographs is evident in this powerful woodcut. Collection, Los Angeles County Museum of Art. Gift of Clifford Odets.*
5 *Grainy but sharply incised lines, vivid black and white shapes and richly textured areas are characteristic of the traditionally carved woodcut. These typical features are noted in the details from Richard Wiegmann's* Limited Perspective.

5

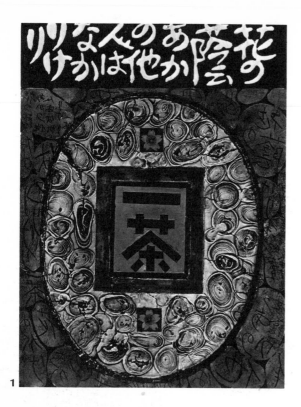

1

THE INTAGLIO PROCESS — ETCHING

The printmaker produces his design on a metal plate, usually zinc or copper, by making lines and scratches down in the plate. This can be done with acid (etching) or scratching (drypoint) or removing a thin V-shaped strip with a burin (engraving). Ink is forced down into these grooves or channels by rubbing, and the unmarked part of the plate is wiped clean. A sheet of dampened paper is placed on the incised plate and the two are run through an etching press which exerts great pressure. The dampened paper is forced down into the grooves and picks up ink that was left there in the wiping. The resulting print is actually a paper mold of the plate, as the printed lines now stand above the surface of the paper. However, the print was obtained by gathering ink from the engraved or etched lines *below* the surface of the metal plate—hence, intaglio.

1 Issa. *Shiro Ikegawa, color intaglio, (29⁷/₈ x 22¹/₈). This print contains examples of various contemporary techniques in intaglio printing, including rich embossing of the surface. Collection, Los Angeles County Museum of Art. Gift of the Container Corporation of America.*
2 The Prodigal Son Among Swine. *Albrecht Dürer, line engraving (9³/₄ x 7¹/₂). Countless fine lines have been engraved into the copper plate for this detailed print in which all dark shaded areas have been produced by massing of thin lines. Collection, Los Angeles County Museum of Art.*
3 St. Jerome in an Italian Landscape. *Rembrandt van Rijn, etching and drypoint, (10¹/₄ x 8¹/₄). Rembrandt was a master at using chiaroscuro in both painting and his etched plates. Dark areas are produced by continual cross-hatching. Collection, Los Angeles County Museum of Art.*
4 Battle of the Eleven Knights. *Malcolm Myers, intaglio, (17³/₄ x 23¹/₂). This contemporary printmaker used deeply etched lines and textures in contrast with a dark textured area. Collection, Los Angeles County Museum of Art. Gift of Otis Art Associates.*
5 *The use of fine lines, cross-hatching and a shaded pattern of tiny white dots on a dark surface are characteristic of traditional intaglio prints. Detail from Piazza Publico by the author.*
6 Facade, 1963. *Arthur Thrall, intaglio, (22¹/₂ x 17). Done in etching and aquatint technique, the print assumes the feeling of a woodcut, due to the simulated grainy surfaces, providing some ideas for woodcuts done in pieces. Courtesy, Orlando Gallery, Encino, California.*

2

3

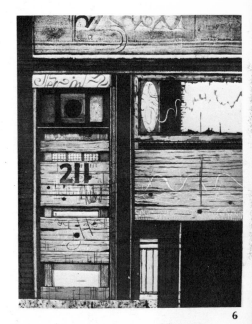

6

4

5

19

THE STENCIL PROCESS — SERIGRAPHY

1

This is the newest of the print media to enter exhibition circles, and it is largely an American development. Its striking feature is the use of many colors which are printed over each other through a series of stencils. These stencils are fixed on separate screens of silk that have been stretched on wooden frames. Each frame is a separate printing unit, with the stencils being made of glue, paper, tusche and glue, or other block-out techniques. Silk-screen paint is put on one end of the frame and is drawn across the silk and stencil with a rubber squeegee. The open parts of the stencil will print in vivid colors while areas blocked out remain clean. With the use of transparent colors, multiple overlapping effects can be achieved. The print is obtained by forcing ink *through* a stencil, thereby differing greatly from other print processes.

A look at a few examples of finished prints will give you an inkling of the feel of each type of work.

2

3

1 And the wind pitched his tent. *Corita Kent serigraph, (19 x 26). Large paper stencils characterize the artist's prints, usually produced in vivid colors. Collection of Fred Parker.*

2 *Brushed glue stencils produce a characteristic surface much like that of a textural painting, as this detail from Impression of Forio by Robert E. Wood shows. Collection of the author.*

3 Wharf Space IV. *Robert E. Wood, serigraph, (19¼ x 27). Patterned shapes created by more than 20 separate stencils produce excellent value contrasts in this print. As in the case of many artists, this print closely resembles Mr. Wood's watercolor paintings. Collection of the author.*

4 Blue Candescence. *Joyce Heimberger, serigraph, (17½ x 29¾). This print is screened in many colors and has a painterly quality produced by using stencils of glue applied to the silk with a brush. Collection, Los Angeles County Museum of Art. Gift of Mr. and Mrs. Oscar Salzer.*

5 Primeval. *Leonard Edmondson, serigraph, (11 x 16¾). All methods of working with silk screen stencils are exhibited in this print. Collection, Los Angeles County Museum of Art. Gift of Mr. and Mrs. Oscar Salzer.*

6 The Whole Duty of Man. *Richard Wiegmann, serigraph, (19 x 14). Cut paper stencils produce hard edge colors in this uniquely shaped print. Collection of the author.*

21

1

THE RELIEF PRINT — SUBTRACTION AND ADDITION

The potential for the relief printmaker is unlimited. Any surface that is irregular in relief and that will retain ink can produce a print. This book lists dozens of ways in which this can be accomplished, but two basic methods of achieving it are evident—one is by subtracting and the other is by addition.

Subtracting from the original surface was, until recent years, the only way of producing a relief print. Woods of various types, linoleum, and some cardboards were used in this process, and certain limitations are evident. There are many kinds of marks that can be made with gouges, chisels and knives, but limits are still present, and printmakers had to work within those limits. Wood can provide different grains and textures, images can be strong or detailed, the artist can use large gouges or small veiners. The process is always similar and the resulting print is clearly anticipated by the experienced printmaker.

It wasn't until recent years that excitement was introduced into the realm of the relief print. With the freeing of various other art forms from the shackles of the past, the 20th century also emancipated the relief print from its stereotyped format. When other media stressed the use of new materials, the relief print was soon to follow. And now by the process of addition, printmakers were ready to place all sorts of foreign materials on their blocks—foreign to traditional printmaking at least. The relief print stepped into the 20th century, although belatedly, and today is enjoying the result of the creative ingenuity of many experimental artists. Look carefully at the examples of the contemporary Japanese printmakers to see the results of such experimentation.

Metals, plastics, glass, paper, wood, masonite, organic materials and many found objects and manufactured things have been worked into wood planks—and from there into relief prints. Working with raw wood, weathered planks, rusted gears, crushed tin cans and broken glass has become part of the printmaker's idiom. Cloth, string, crumpled paper, tools and implements have crept into the printshop.

With these and many other things at his disposal, today's printmaker is an innovator and experimental researcher, providing the world with another look at itself and its products in a way not possible in any other medium.

And when all the thousands of exciting avenues have been explored, and the printmaker has exhausted the material and techniques available in the relief printing medium, he can begin to combine his methods with the serigraph, the lithograph and the intaglio—and this should open a few more doors.

3

4

5

1 Moonlight Marine. *A collagraph that incorporates several materials including wood, string and sand; (16 x 12). Lutheran High School, Los Angeles.*

2 Ancient Writing C. Hiroyuki Tajima, woodcut, (36 x 24). *A handsome print, this contemporary Japanese woodcut makes use of beautifully textured surfaces and the more traditional graded woodcut coloring. The overall appearance is almost that of a tapestry. Courtesy, M. M. Shinno.*

3 *The excellently designed woodcut was printed on two colors of tissue paper with two colors of ink. The two sheets were laminated together, off-register, on a sheet of illustration board. Lutheran High School, Los Angeles.*

4 Nothing touches me . . . in an audience of oblique hate. *Two-color linoleum cut on pelon. (10 x 16). This is a strong statement print and was done by a student at Los Angeles High School.*

5 Cathedral shapes, *printed on tissue paper, laminated to illustration board. The texture of the string can be seen in some places and some lines are doubled by overlapping the 20 by 14 print. Lutheran High School, Los Angeles.*

1

2

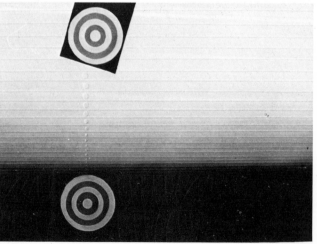

3

1 Sorrowing and Terrified Man. Leonard Baskin, woodcut, (34¹/₂ inch diameter). The artist's work makes use of very delicately cut lines that remain raised to produce thin black lines on the print. These contrast strongly with the large black and white areas. Collection, Pasadena Art Museum, California.
2 Poem 69-44. Haku Maki, woodcut, (10 x 7). The embossed relief areas were printed from cement forms on the wood. The black idiograph of a horse was printed with a wood stamp while the other color was added with a stencil. Courtesy, M. M. Shinno.
3 Recollections. Kunihiro Amano, woodcut, (16 x 24). The colors were printed first, and then the print was deeply embossed. Courtesy, M. M. Shinno.
4 Head of Ludwig Schames. Ernst Ludwig Kirchner, woodcut, (22-15/16 x 10-5/16). Collection, The Museum of Modern Art, New York; Abby Aldrich Rockefeller Fund.

AN APPROACH TO RELIEF PRINTMAKING

Highly important to the print is its technique, and printmaking can only be fully appreciated through understanding and experience with the medium. The skills required are important because a good print is the result of a thorough knowledge of tools and materials and the best way to use them.

As important as it is to understand the traditional techniques and procedures in producing a woodcut or linoleum cut, it is just as important that a feeling of exploration pervades the print classroom. To be sure, there is suspense and surprise with the pulling of the first linoleum print. There should also be the surprise of discovery—discovery of a new and different shape or a new color to print or an exquisite natural texture or a combination of forms and shapes in multi-color.

The key to good teaching in this period of stress on exploration is balance. We have to encourage experimentation but we also must teach fundamentals. The inquisitive student should know something of the traditional approaches, because only then can he use them for the strength they possess in combination with more experimental techniques. If the foundation is not present, then the experiments are achieved in a vacuum and are merely a series of attempts, not fitting into any context of continuity with the entire medium. This book is set up that way—the linoleum cut and woodcut, followed by a multitude of departures, but always carried out in the context of the entire printmaking spectrum.

In years gone by the word "printmaking" conjured up the image of a nearsighted little old man carving wood and inking blocks in an ink-stained studio. In recent years it has come to mean something else—a researching, experimenting, exploring artist whose studio contains a variety of electric tools, large sheets of plywood, masonite and cardboard, and boxes full of metal, plastic and machined parts.

A change is taking place in all the art world, and printmaking is not exempt from this change. Like painting or sculpture, printmaking should mean an exposure to new experiences, the privilege to attempt new ways of saying things. The printmaker has a fantastic range of new materials with which to work, and with the introduction of built-up surfaces to produce prints he can make valuable explorations in color, design, movement and optical effects.

Printmaking answers the desire to work with materials in a different way, and an inborn interest in tools that most of us have. Instead of deftly twirling a bristle brush loaded with acrylic juice, or craftily putting down a weighted line with charcoal, print-

4

making is almost literally something to sink your teeth into. (Might make a nice impression on a woodcut.) The manipulation of tools and equipment is intriguing to teenagers and the boldness with which the block may be attacked is a vital and exciting experience.

The carving of a line calls for different motions of the body and hand than the painting of a line with watercolor. The knife must be grabbed firmly and drawn toward the body. The gouge is also held firmly and driven down and away from the body along the grain of wood. The use of some physical strength is appealing to most young people, and here again printmaking helps provide an outlet.

The print must speak for itself. It dare not try to be a painting, for the quality of the brush, paint and color is not usually obtainable in a print. It dare not try to be a drawing, because the subtle variations of tone cannot be achieved in wood. It must be what it is—a print. And, at that, no other medium can approach it.

The printing surface is not plastic, nor can it reflect anything but what the block provides. A successful print must depend on the power of its design and the handling of the tools. The character of the print and the strokes it records should come from the knife and gouge and from the feel of the blade as it cuts through the material.

The work on the block should be as free as possible, because too much planning and calculation not only makes it difficult to cut but will tend to destroy the enjoyment of working.

The woodcut should look like a woodcut. It should bear witness to the struggle between printmaker and block and should echo that struggle in ink. The boldness and decisiveness of the cutter should give character to the print. Don't try to make the woodcut look like a linoleum print—smooth and even. And don't spend excess time trying to grain a linoleum block to look like wood. Use each material the best way it can be used, working it as vigorously and as honestly as possible. Remember, the character of the print is a direct reflection of the process that produces it. Let the print be a print!

Too often the prints coming from art rooms are small black and white linoleum cuts that have nothing at all in common with the important prints and innovations in today's art. Glance through this book and see what's happening today—reflect on the trends and fascinating approaches to the relief print. No student should be excluded from the wondrous and exhilarating experiences of today's relief printing methods.

2

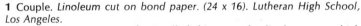

4

5

1 Couple. *Linoleum cut on bond paper. (24 x 16). Lutheran High School, Los Angeles.*

2 Marina Movement. *Jo Rebert pulled this two-color linoleum cut which is 14 x 20 in size. Her design is similar to her painting technique.*

3 Fantasy in Red. *Hideo Hagiwara, woodcut, (24 x 36). Because of the many separate blocks used and the numerous overprintings, this woodcut has a surface that is rich in texture and color variations. Courtesy, M. M. Shinno.*

4 *Linoleum cut made by cutting the lines that are printed black into the block. The block was inked with white water soluble ink and printed on white paper, and when dry was covered with india ink. When the ink dried, the paper was rinsed off under a spray of water which removed all the white inked areas including the india ink that was on it. The india ink remains fixed to the paper in the remaining areas, showing as black lines on a white surface. Print by Lois McMillan.*

5 *Three woodcuts that show the characteristics of the wood and the rugged simplicity desirable in the woodcut technique. Lutheran High School, Los Angeles.*

A MATTER OF DESIGN

Preoccupation with materials must not become the only reason for producing a print, although some experimental prints that deal primarily with found objects will require little in the way of planning. But a print which is created in the absence of some design principles or an understanding of the elements of art is like a house built of bricks but no mortar—there is nothing to hold it together.

A small space here will be given to the matter of design but will not be reiterated in each chapter. Nor should the printmaking class become one which deals in the problems of design. Individual teacher and student conferences during class are the best places to remind, influence and cause the young artist to understand these principles—right in the context of his current work.

Some methods of working contained in this book deal more with one element of art than another—line, shape, texture, color and value are touched on in nearly all of them.

The writhing *line* of the string print, the incised line of the linoleum cut, the delicate grainy line of a piece of weathered wood, the accidental lines created by crumpled paper, the jagged lines that a gouge makes in wood, and the almost invisible lines in the veins of a leaf print are all vital experiences in using line. Calling attention to the quality, variety and strength of these many lines will cause students to become more familiar with them and use them more readily in working with other media.

Shapes, both positive and negative, are the structure of most woodcuts—strong and dynamic, rounded and monolithic, or jagged and stringy. The linoleum cut, the collagraph, the cardboard print or the experimental prints with natural and found forms will contribute to the student's vocabulary of shapes. The shapes of the repeat design printed with an eraser are important, as they must work together in their repetitive context. Shape and line must work together in almost every kind of print.

Texture is one of the natural results of printmaking. While the linoleum print must be textured on purpose or otherwise remain flat, most other materials worked with will carry their own textures to the print. Wood, textiles, wire mesh, screen, string, rope, pebbled mat board, corrugated cardboard, leaves, sandpaper, crumpled paper and other materials add to the textured richness of our prints. And where the textures do not exist, they are simulated by gouging, nailing, scratching, tearing, drilling, gluing or working the material one way or another.

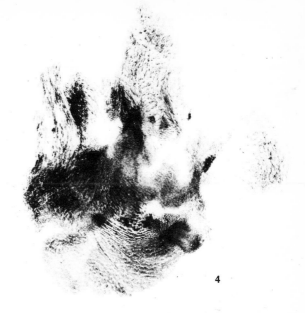

4

5

1 White Night. *R. Mizufune, woodcut, (20 x 24). The artist used ten colors of heavily applied ink to produce this print, which has a surface texture that is almost painterly. Courtesy, M. M. Shinno.*
2 Couple. *Woodcut, (15 x 11¹/₂). Several strong shapes carry the message in this print. Lutheran High School, Los Angeles.*
3 *Intricately textured woodcut surface that was prepared by burning with alcohol and wire brushing out the charred parts. Work is by Pat Obey.*
4 *The textures of a printed elbow are varied and actually beautiful.*
5 *Design produced by inking the punched metal grille and bits of fiber glass from a furnace filter.*

MAY WEBER

1

Color is not inherent in relief printing, since one color might easily be used to great advantage—and often that one color is black. Contemporary printmakers have found that color can be used to great advantage, and today's print shows are visual explosions in color. Overprinting several colors, especially if textures are involved, can produce dazzling textural effects. Some printing methods explained in this book will allow for full use of color, and some photographed examples, though printed in black, grays and white were made with brilliant color combinations. While the silkscreen technique has generally been the realm of color in printmaking, other methods today are stealing much of that thunder.

Stressing *value* in most woodcuts or linoleum prints is not necessary, since black and white allows little area for value study. Some artists have tried to grade the elevation of the block with sandpaper to produce gray areas. But generally speaking, the woodcut and linoleum cut do not deal much in value. If value is important to the print subject, it can often be obtained by stippling or other methods that pick out various-sized pieces of the block. The collagraph, however, does require an arrangement of the many variations in dark and light to project its image, and this is controlled to a great extent by the wiping process. The changing of a value drawing or photograph to pure black and white for a woodcut design does require a working facility with value variations, so that even here, a practical knowledge of value is necessary.

Individual problems in design, or the arrangement of the parts of the print, will normally be covered in personal talks with each student. The teacher can offer suggestions regarding *balance* in a woodcut design, or *rhythm* in the repeated forms of an eraser print, or *emphasis* in the collagraph plate, or *variety* of forms and textures in the linoleum cut, or the *unity* required to tie the parts of a cardboard print together, or the *movement* needed to make an ordinary glue print exciting. The students should be made aware of these essential principles, but they should not be allowed to dominate the activity—that is left to the design classes. The real balance is one between feeling and principles—between subject matter and technique. In printmaking the principles of design should be used like reins, allowing the students to move up and away at their individual speeds, keeping them down to earth with a few reminders and checks now and then.

1 A Man Reading. Max Weber, color woodcut, (9³/₄ x 6¹/₄). *The artist arranged to have spaces left between his colors, thus eliminating the need for close registration. Collection, The Museum of Modern Art, New York; Abby Aldrich Rockefeller Fund.*
2 New Landscape No. 2. Hideo Hagiwara, woodcut, (36 x 24). *With yellows, oranges and browns dominating the print, the artist has combined large flat areas, smaller textural treatments, and rhythmic lines in a fascinating display of contemporary printmaking techniques. Courtesy, M. M. Shinno.*
3 Iceberg. *Linoleum cut emphasizing large shapes contrasted with delicate detail. (14 x 9). Courtesy, Lutheran High School, Los Angeles.*
4 S. No. 10. Rikio Takahashi, color woodcut, (6 x 8). *Pieces of wood, printed with transparent inks, produce a series of beautiful overlays. Courtesy, M. M. Shinno.*

30

4

1

2

3

THE LINOLEUM CUT

Probably the most common and best known of all relief printing methods is the linoleum print. And it is very possible that the commonness of this medium has caused it to be underestimated as a fine art technique. It is a shame that most people immediately associate "linoleum prints" with "homemade greeting cards." Although ideally suited for this duplicating process, linoleum cuts can stand on their own as well-accepted prints among the various contemporary printmaking techniques. Developed around either representational or nonobjective subject matter, and in one or more colors, they are today as highly respected as their more sophisticated printmaking counterparts: the woodcut, the lithograph, the intaglio or the serigraph.

It is true that linoleum cuts are excellent for producing illustrations for the school newspaper, or making bookplates, or menu covers, or greeting cards, or repeat designs for wrapping paper, but their use is not restricted to such "practical" purposes. Especially when larger sized sheets of the material are employed, linoleum cuts can become an exciting and handsome printmaking technique.

Pablo Picasso and Henri Matisse have done much to enhance the honor of the linoleum cut, with Picasso executing a large series of linoleum color prints in the years 1958 to 1963. Its advantages as a printmaking material should be explored in every art room, since it is easy to cut in any direction, is excellent for working with clean hard edges, and is superb when working with a variety of colors.

Linoleum is a living material. It is soft and dull when new, but hardens and shines with constant use, especially when absorbing

4

1 Olivera Street. *Jo Rebert, linoleum cut in three colors, (22 x 30).*
2 February. *Carmen Terrazas, linoleum cut, (20 x 24). Spirit of excitement is generated in this seemingly complex single color print. Collection, Lois McMillan.*
3 Toros y Toreros. *Pablo Picasso, linoleum cut, (12 x 14¹/₂). Two colors were used by the artist in this print accomplished through the elimination process described later in the text. Courtesy, London Arts Gallery, Detroit, Michigan.*
4 Child of the World. *This 18 x 24 linoleum cut has a beautifully worked surface, and shows excellent use of texture contrasted with solid areas. Los Angeles High School.*

33

1

oils from the printing inks. The friction of burnishing also increases the hardness and polish of the surface to make it look like old leather. It can be a pleasure to handle and work when in this state.

MATERIALS TO USE

Linoleum comes in a variety of forms but not all are desirable in the classroom. Battleship linoleum is excellent and is available from dealers in light solid colors (which are best) or in dark colors which can be lightened if necessary by painting with white tempera or acrylic paint. A creamy white battleship linoleum is available which is used commercially in covering drafting tables. The inlaid types of the material, or vinyl squares, are extremely hard and difficult to cut and should be avoided.

Scraps of battleship linoleum can be purchased from some dealers, or large rolls can be ordered from major suppliers. It can either be felt-backed or burlap-backed, with the former being easier to cut up into pieces and also more reasonable. If purchased in large rolls, it has a tendency to hold the curvature of the roll for a long time. Therefore, it is advantageous to cut off some large sections and flatten them, to be cut up into required sizes later on.

The sheets or rolls of linoleum can be cut to a variety of shapes and sizes to fit the subject or the desire of the students. Cutting can be done with a sharp mat knife and a large metal square or straightedge on the back of the material. A few strokes of the knife and the linoleum can be bent over a table edge and cleanly broken on the scored line. Big pieces can also be cut into smaller sizes with a large paper cutter.

These pieces can be worked on as they now are or they can be mounted on plywood or masonite if desired. If the new linoleum seems too soft, place it on the floor and walk and stomp on it. This will make it harder and often easier to work—that is, if minor scratches will not harm the overall design of the intended block.

Linoleum can also be purchased in an already mounted state, type high (7/8 inch high) and ready to work. There are limits imposed, however, as to sizes available and the expense of the larger-sized mounted blocks.

2

1 Blues Singer. *Lois McMillan, linoleum cut, (12 x 16).*
2 *Linoleum comes in large rolls or in blocks with the battleship linoleum already glued to type high pieces of plywood.*
3 Star of Persia II. *Frank Stella, lithograph, (26 x 32). Simple form and color characterize the strong work of the artist, characteristics also vital to the printing of linoleum blocks. Collection, Los Angeles County Museum of Art. Lent by Mr. and Mrs. David Gensburg.*
4 *The problem was to illustrate a line from a poem, and also print that line. The illustration was done in linoleum, 8 x 6 inches, and the lettering was printed from cutout cardboard letters, adhered to a cardboard backing. Lutheran High School, Los Angeles.*
5 *Contemporary advertising techniques might be readily applicable to some phases of linoleum block printing. This 26 x 18 print features a two-piece musical group. Lutheran High School, Los Angeles.*
6 Man. *Two-color linoleum cut with abstract background block overprinted with black portrait print, 18 x 16. Los Angeles High School.*

3

...but the children are burning in vietnam

4

FRESH CREAM

5

6

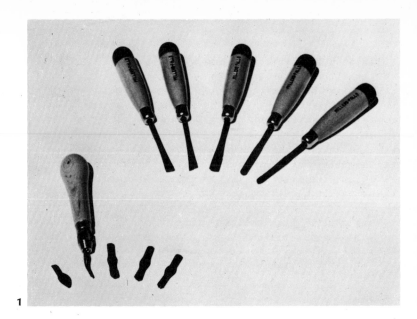

1

2

3

4

There is nothing weak or limiting about the linoleum block as far as numbers of prints are concerned. Records show that 2,500 to 3,000 prints have been successfully pulled from a single block. Students will not require this number of prints, but any block will supply the student artist with as many prints as he will need.

If very fine lines or details are required in the print, the surface of the linoleum may be scraped with the flat of a razor blade, or may be sanded with the finest grade of "wet and dry" sandpaper available. Excellent working surfaces can be obtained in both of these ways—normal printmaking will not require either of these steps.

If the linoleum gets too hard to cut easily in the coldness of winter, it can be placed near a warm stove or in the sun for a while. This will make it more receptive to the cutting action that must follow.

TOOLS

Any of a variety of linoleum cutting tools can be used to cut the block. There are both push and pull types of cutters, with the more traditional push types being more popular. Gouges, both wide and narrow, veiners making small and large V-shaped markings, and knives are the basic tools. Some come with fixed handles while others are in sets, with one handle and several cutters that can be affixed to the handle. Knives may vary from mat knives and X-acto sets to very sharp pocket knives.

Linoleum cutting tools should be kept very sharp, since they tend to dull rather quickly against the grit contained in the linoleum. Actually, they dull faster working with linoleum than with wood. Sharpening stones (for the backs and edges of tools) and slipstones (for inside the gouges) are practical in keeping the knives at correct sharpness. The fingernail test is best for checking sharpness. If the tool slips when being run over the thumbnail, sharpen it until, on another try, it catches. Dull tools will cut linoleum, but usually after sliding and cutting several unwanted lines or the non-cutting hand. The feel of a sharp gouge cutting linoleum is both pleasurable and satisfying, and leads to a greater desire on the part of the student to experiment and try various textures and lines.

5

1 *Linoleum cutters come in two varieties. The set above comes with handles affixed to each type of cutter, while the set below has exchangeable blades. Both sets include veiners, gouges, and a cutting knife.*
2 Bright Eyes. *Roger Hollenbeck, serigraph, (6^1/$_2$ x 12). Although not a linoleum cut, this print shows an excellent use of simple shapes to produce an exciting design. Collection, Pasadena Art Museum, California. Gift of Mr. and Mrs. Oscar Salzer.*
3 *Slipstone (left) and sharpening stone should be used often and carefully to keep the linoleum cutting tools in best working conditions.*
4 Gentle Wind. *The single color 24 x 14 inch linoleum print shows excellent cutting technique, especially in developing the flowing feeling in the hair. Lutheran High School, Los Angeles.*
5 *Excellent cutting technique and an expressionistic graphic portrayal are evident in this 24 x 18 inch linoleum cut. Los Angeles High School.*

PROCEDURES TO FOLLOW

It is best to precede the actual cutting experience with a few days of preliminary work. Students should work in black and white for a while, a method best carried out with brush and ink on paper—learning to think in black and white. Several sketches followed by one or two finished black and white brush drawings might well introduce the unit on linoleum prints.

After subject matter is chosen (and this might be checked by the art teacher for suitability to the printmaking techniques) it should be stated with black ink or felt-tipped pen directly on the light colored linoleum. Student artists should be encouraged to work with large simple shapes at first, and when more familiar with the cutting techniques, they can work with as much detail as their designs call for.

Students may also work their designs out in pencil, transfer them to the blocks with carbon paper, and then india ink the blocks to show light and dark patterns. If no carbon paper is available, a soft pencil rubbed on the reverse side of the paper will act as carbon when applying the design to the block.

Remember that the block will print in reverse, in a mirror image, and if lettering is involved, or if the design *needs* to face a certain direction, it must be put on the block backwards from the way the finished product should read. This can be done by drawing the design on bond or tracing paper the way it should finally appear. Holding the drawing against an outside window or over a light table, go over the lines on the back of the paper. This reversed drawing should then be transferred to the block, brushed in with india ink, and the work is ready to proceed.

The white areas of the india-inked block should then be cut away—these are the areas that will remain white on the final print. A small V-shaped tool, called a veiner, might take away the initial outline of the white areas and larger gouges can remove bigger areas of white. Keep the non-cutting hand out of danger—even behind the cutting blade, to hold the block firm. A bench hook might also be used to hold the block in place while cutting. Knives and other tools can be used to produce textures of various types but these should be used in conjunction with larger masses of black and white. Cut away white areas until a feeling of completeness is approached. Experiment with types of line and textures, trying to create a variety of surfaces. Have an extra block or two available for trying out textural ideas.

1 Learn to think, with brush and ink, on paper, before beginning to work on the blocks.
2 Working in strong black and white shapes can be done with felt-tipped marker as well as with brush and ink.
3 Transferring the brush and ink design to a sheet of linoleum, using india ink to blacken the block prior to cutting.
4 Using the bench hook to keep the left hand out of the way of the cutter. A board, like the one holding the linoleum block in place, is nailed on one end of the plywood slab, facing down. When hooked over the edge of the table, it keeps the unit from "traveling".

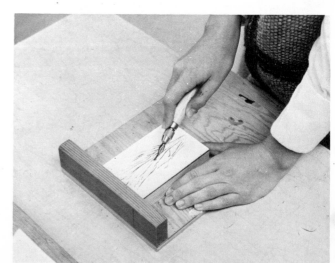

5

6

7

5 Brush and ink studies made prior to inking on the blocks. These were made by re-drawing newspaper photographs and eliminating the middle values, inking only the dark values and leaving the rest white. Lutheran High School, Los Angeles.

6 Interesting print, with cubist overtones, makes excellent use of a wide variety of textures. This 12 by 9 print is from South Hills High School, Pittsburgh, Pennsylvania. Courtesy, Section on Art, Pittsburgh Schools.

7 The mirror effect of the block print is shown with the design on the left (on the block) being prepared in an opposite direction from the print on the right (on the paper). The linoleum on the left is mounted on a type high (0.918 inch) block of plywood. Roosevelt High School, Los Angeles.

39

1 Any Harbor in a Storm. *Linoleum cut printed with dark blue ink on green watercolor-stained rice paper, (10 x 12). Baltimore City Schools, Maryland.*

2 *Rugged and massive shapes can be produced in linoleum as well as wood, as this 18 by 12 print shows. It was inked in black and printed on brown paper. South Hills High School, Pittsburgh, Pennsylvania. Courtesy, Section on Art, Pittsburgh Schools.*

3 *Wide range of textural applications feature this exciting linoleum block and they are further enhanced by large solid areas; 16 x 14 in size. Los Angeles High School.*

4 Double Figure. *Kazumi Amano, woodcut, (36 x 24). This large woodcut was done in six colors and relies on repeating forms, large and bold on the outside and echoed by the subtle shapes in the interior. Courtesy, M. M. Shinno.*

5 *Ink usually comes in tubes, as at left. The materials on the right include a jar of water-soluble oil and several containers of powdered pigment and a canister of powdered tempera. These powders and the oil are mixed with the palette knife on the glass slab, then rolled up with the brayer and applied to the block.*

6 *Water based printing ink, four types of brayers, and a glass sheet for rolling out the ink prior to inking the block.*

7 *Sometimes a successful print can be made by simply cutting out the lines and printing. This decorative print was done in blue ink, and is 14 inches square. Lutheran High School, Los Angeles.*

40

5

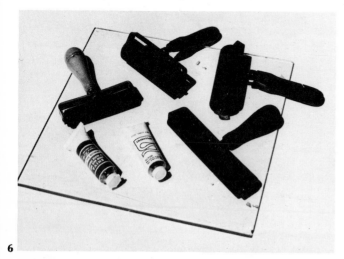

6

7

PROOFING THE BLOCK

Roll up some black ink with a brayer on an ink slab and apply it to the block. Using a piece of newsprint and rubbing the inked block with a spoon, the first sample proof might then be pulled. Check the print. Analyze it and be ready to do some more cutting and texturing as needed. To see if more white would look better in some areas, place small bits of newsprint on the print to check the appearance. Continue cutting and printing proofs until satisfied with the product, then get ready to pull the prints required for the edition.

PRINTING THE BLOCK

Basic tools and materials necessary for printing the final edition include ink, ink slab, brayer, paper and some type of pressure to transfer the ink from the block to the paper.

THE INKS

Both oil and water soluble inks are satisfactory when printing linoleum blocks. Other things being equal, the water based products are easier to clean in the art room, dry more quickly and might therefore be a bit more satisfactory.

One-color prints should generally be inked in black or a dark shade, unless the subject or use requires another color. Both oil and water soluble inks come in a range of basic colors, which can be mixed on the ink slab for still greater variety.

A water soluble oil is available that can be mixed with dry pigments or dry tempera to produce an infinite variety of colors. The pigments are added to the oil on the ink slab, mixed with a palette knife, rolled up with the brayer and applied to the block. Tools can be cleaned with water. See chapter 9 for additional information.

THE INK SLAB

A sheet of plate glass, about 10 x 10 inches, makes an excellent ink slab. The edges should be ground smooth at the glass shop or they should be covered with masking tape to prevent the cutting of fingers. A sheet of formica or metal might also serve as an ink slab.

THE BRAYER

Linoleum printing requires either a hard or soft rubber brayer, with the former being more inexpensive and certainly as serviceable. Soft rubber brayers are best for inking woodcuts because they will adapt to the varying elevations of the carved relief, but since linoleum blocks are smooth and even, the hard rubber brayers are satisfactory.

Brayers should be cleaned well after use, especially when using oil-based inks, since the unused ink will dry and cake on the roller, causing uneven inking of future prints.

Linoleum blocks can also be inked with stiff bristle brushes or a leather dabber.

Care should be taken in cleaning the rubber brayers that have wooden cores in them, as the wood will swell on the ends when wet. This will distort the rubber so that the center of the roller won't touch the surface of the plate to pick up the ink. Do not let them soak in water or hold them for long periods of time under running water when cleaning. A bit of water and a damp paper towel or cloth will do the trick.

PAPER

Papers of a wide variety should be available to the printmaking students so they can experiment and decide which best fits their subject and use. Final prints should be made on a paper that will stand the abuse of rubbing with a spoon or being subjected to a press, and yet accept the ink readily. This might be a bond paper, white drawing paper, construction paper (any color), oatmeal paper, or some of the more reasonable rice papers or imitation rice papers. A medium weight pelon, available at yardage shops, comes in wide rolls and can be purchased by the yard. The waxless variety is best and will produce excellent prints when spooned. Classes wanting to work on large prints (12 x 18 inches and larger) should try this material as a printing surface. Search out new and different papers—they can lend excitement to the printing experience. See chapters 3 and 9 for more information on paper.

PULLING THE PRINT

With the finished block, a stack of printing paper, a brayer, an ink slab, ink and a spoon, the young printmaker is ready to produce his edition. The prepared ink can be squeezed or placed on the edge of the glass and rolled up on the ink slab, with the brayer—until the roller is evenly coated. Roll the brayer in several directions on the glass, lifting it from time to time to insure an even coverage of ink. The ink is then transferred to the block by rolling over it in several directions until it is evenly covered. The correct amount is a matter of trial and error and will be determined with a bit of experience. Too little ink will leave a grayed image (which might be very pleasing) and too much ink will fill the small cutout areas and print too thickly, causing drying difficulties and a loss of detail.

1 *Inking a large linoleum sheet with the brayer.*
2 *Black Is. Linoleum cut printed with black ink on brown kraft paper, (24 x 18). Use contemporary and meaningful themes to involve students in the subject matter of the print. Los Angeles High School.*
3 *Several linear patterned blocks, when overprinted, can produce some intricate textures. This linoleum cut, 12 by 11½ in size, is from Allegheny High School, Pittsburgh, Pennsylvania. Courtesy, Section on Art, Pittsburgh Schools.*
4 *Wooden spoon, a baren or a smooth rounded stone can all be used to burnish the printing paper to produce a print.*
5 *Using a wood spoon to burnish a linoleum cut, transferring the ink from block to paper.*
6 *Using a baren to apply pressure in printing a linoleum cut.*

1

2

3

4

5

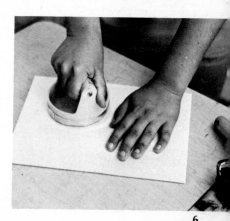

6

1

2

3

With the inked block facing up, place the paper, several inches larger than the block, down on the surface and give it a quick rub with the hand to simply keep it stuck in place. Then either rub the back of the paper with a wooden spoon, smooth flat stone or a baren. A metal spoon might also be used, but friction causes quite a bit of heat and discomfort while rubbing. The baren is a hand-held tool, designed for use in printing woodcuts, and is discussed in chapter 3. The block might also be run through a press, if one is available, but the rubbing technique (burnishing) is considered the best. While burnishing, check occasionally to see if the print is being transferred fully to the paper, and if not, re-ink where needed and continue the burnishing process.

If a rice paper-like material is used, the ink will show through it during the rubbing and the printmaker will be able to check the coverage without lifting the edge of the print. When finished, pull the print and hang it up to dry, either with clothespins on a rack or pinned to a wall with tacks or pins. Prints may also be stacked carefully between sheets of blotting paper but should not be stacked on top of each other directly, because they will smudge easily until they are dry.

Another method of applying pressure is to run a clean, dry brayer over the printing paper. This is not as effective as burnishing, but can produce adequate results. Pressure can also be exerted by standing on the block, placed face down on the printing paper with a pad of newspaper underneath. This is simply known as the foot press, and excellent results can be obtained in this way. Pressure can also be applied to small prints by carefully beating with a wooden or plastic mallet. Linoleum cuts might also be run through a washing machine wringer.

Prints from linoleum cuts appear as a reverse image of the block —a mirror reflection. This might be a bit disconcerting at first, since so much time has been spent working on the block in its original orientation. Actually, the reverse image will lend itself to a more open critical analysis on the part of the student.

Print an edition of five or more so some might be exchanged with classmates. When dry, the edition should be titled, numbered and signed. See chapter 9 for details regarding this concluding process. The printing is then finished.

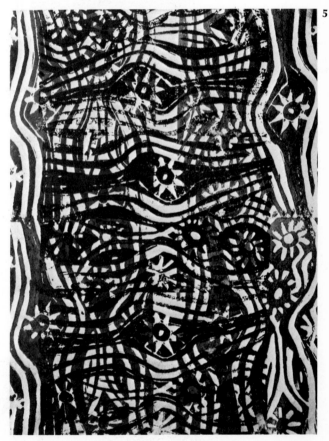

1 *Textural background obtained by printing the image lightly (with a partially dry brayer for inking) upside down, and printing over that with a fully inked block right side up. The block is 12 x 9 and was printed at Lutheran High School, Los Angeles.*
2 *The first glimpse of the burnished print is always exciting. This one was done on a rice paper-like material that allows the ink to show through the print when it is being rubbed.*
3 *Pulling the burnished print in a trial proof. The student artist is trying to see what the print will look like if not printed in its full length. He used the ink bottle on the table as a burnisher.*
4 *Design for a calendar in which the background shape is a brayer print, the camel is a linoleum cut, the straws are printed with a stamp, and the lettering is silkscreened. Bancroft Junior High School, Los Angeles.*
5 *An uneven repeat pattern printed in one color vertically and a second color horizontally, (11 1/2 x 8 1/2). Baltimore City Schools, Maryland.*

MORE THAN ONE COLOR?

Producing prints of more than one color is sometimes desirable but remember that it is time consuming and often simply a lesson in perseverance. In most cases with student artists, more can be learned by making two single color prints than one two-color or three-color print.

Before we go into several conventional ways to produce multi-color prints, here are a few ways to add color, variety and spice to the printing without much effort but with maximum excitement and stimulation.

The single block can be printed in two values of the same color. Print first with a light value, using a lightly-inked brayer or by adding white ink to the glass slab. Then invert the block and print again (upside down or sideways) with a dark value or black. This will not always work out well, but very often produces some wonderful, fresh shapes and patterns.

If many blocks are the same size, the student can borrow a neighbor's block, print it in one color and print his own block over it with black or a dark value. Or several blocks and several colors can precede the final dark block, or perhaps all should be left as bright color and texture, without the key dark block printed over it. The variety of fascinating patterns and textures is endless.

A third way to get a multicolor print from a single block is to print lightly first and then dark again, but slightly off-register—either right, left, above, below, or diagonally. This usually produces an instant shadow effect and some wonderful repeated shapes. Experiment with different distances and colors. Or, place the second block side by side with the first print and perhaps repeat for three prints—instant repetitious patterns. Again, not all blocks lend themselves to these treatments, but if they do, very exciting bonus results can occur.

Another easy variation would be to print a texture from a slab of wood and print the linoleum block over that. Or roll a nearly

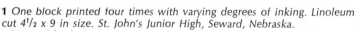

1 *One block printed four times with varying degrees of inking. Linoleum cut 4¹/₂ x 9 in size. St. John's Junior High, Seward, Nebraska.*
2 *Textural background was printed in light value color upside down, and overprinted in dark value right side up. Only one 18 x 14 linoleum plate was used in printing. Lutheran High School, Los Angeles.*
3 *The same block, printed in three different directions and with three varying amounts of ink, can provide some wonderful abstract patterns. Inked block can be blotted to provide the lesser intense values. Linoleum cut is 7 x 6 in size. St. John's Junior High, Seward, Nebraska.*
4 *Octopus. Three-color linoleum cut in magenta and purple with a yellow eye; 10 x 12 in size. Los Angeles High School.*
5 *The single linoleum cut was printed in black on light green tissue paper and in white on dark green tissue paper. Pieces of the former print were lacquered to illustration board first, then the entire second print was lacquered over this collage, allowing part of the dark print to show through in places. The print is 24 x 18. Lutheran High School, Los Angeles.*
6 *Feeling of movement is created by printing a second color in lighter value ink over the first print in dark value ink. Some areas of overlapping produce a third color, while the general feeling of agitation provides the sense of movement. This linoleum cut is 24 x 18. Lutheran High School, Los Angeles.*

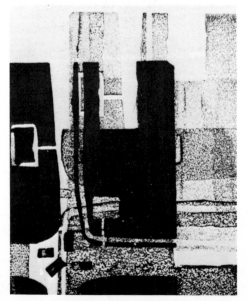

46

4

5

6

47

dry brayer over a sheet of paper to make a light colored area, and print the block on top of this. Prints can also be made on brightly colored tissue paper collages or on a tempera painted surface. The textural surfaces of wallpapers can be underprinted providing an interesting background for a strong print.

Students can come up with some wonderful innovations, if they know they aren't restricted to just the one printing method. Actually the variety of types of prints is only restricted by the creative attitudes of the students in the class. It is often rewarding to have several prints turned in at the end of the unit, one regular print and several experimental additions. And the key word in printmaking today is "experimental."

The more traditional multi-colored print techniques also approach the problem from various points of view and offer a number of solutions, although they might not appear immediately as exciting and attractive as the more experimental approaches. Only a few will be presented here.

The actual cutting of the blocks remains the same, but the difference between a one-color print and a two-color print is in the planning stage. Three basic approaches are evident. One involves a key block, usually the final black print, used in conjunction with one or several color blocks. The second suggests that the final print is made up of several color blocks, each contributing to the final whole. A third method would involve printing several colors from the same block. Each artist must determine which method or combination of methods best suits his needs.

The third method would be the easiest to try, since only one

4

block is required. It might be done by rolling several areas of the block in various colors, or by applying the colored inks with a brush to local areas. It can also be accomplished in the Edward Munch style, by cutting the block in pieces, like a jigsaw puzzle, and inking each part a different color, then placing the pieces back together and printing. This is probably best accomplished if the linoleum is adhered to a backing of plywood or masonite, then placing the cutout pieces in a chase or wooden frame, to hold them rigid while spooning or running through a press. (See woodcut section for illustrations of this technique.)

The simplest of the multi-block prints can be carried out by

1 *Background in this print was made by inking a textured piece of scrap wallpaper and printing it, prior to printing the animal design.*
2 *Madonna. Lois McMillan, linoleum cut, 14 x 10. Printed in black ink on a collage of colored tissue paper mounted on illustration board.*
3 *The three colors in this 24 x 18 print were applied to a single linoleum plate and printed at one time. Los Angeles High School.*
4 *Two treatments of the same linoleum plate produce completely different feelings in the finished product. The print on the left is a regular black print on white paper. The print on the right was printed with a dark ink and a light ink on two separate sheets of tissue paper. These sheets were then adhered to illustration board with lacquer; the light print on top slightly off register. The print is 24 x 18. Lutheran High School, Los Angeles.*
5 *Lion. Three-color linoleum cut with simple background shapes over-printed with handsomely cut key block, 15 x 10¹/₂. Los Angeles High School.*

5

1

2

3

1 Ocelot. Three-color linoleum cut in gold, brown and orange. (12 x 16).
Los Angeles High School.
2 Three-color print in orange and browns was pulled from three separate
blocks. The linoleum cut is 10 x 12. Los Angeles High School.
3 Marina San Pedro. Jo Rebert, two-color linoleum cut, (20 x 28). Strong
shapes and varied line weight are combined with excellent sense of design. Two colors were printed from two separate blocks.
4 Three-color linoleum cut in two light colors and a key block in black.
Eagle Rock High School, Los Angeles.
5 Untitled. Two-color linoleum cut featuring lettering as a method of
expression, (18 x 12). Los Angeles High School.

placing one or several trial prints on newsprint and, using water-color or wash, painting a number of ideas on the trial prints. Then pull a fresh print, and while still wet, press it face down on a second block of linoleum, cut the same size as the key block. When this transferred print dries, the cutting may be done to correspond to the shapes required, by using the watercolored sample as a guide. One- or two-color blocks can be made, or one block can be printed in several directions with several colors for additional background and texture. Now when dry, print the key block over this background. Usually a dark value is best for the key block print—it will tend to pull the design together.

Another traditional method of making multicolored prints would involve more careful planning, as each segment of color needs to be cut on a different block and registered carefully when printing. This procedure is best started by making a line drawing on tracing paper and placing it, with carbon paper, on each of the blocks to be used, one for each color. After deciding which part of the print should be green, cut one block to print this color; another to print the blue, and so on until all the blocks are produced. The final block, printed in a dark value, should tie the entire print together. Consideration should be made for overlapping hues producing a third color.

Care needs to be taken in printing these blocks for accurate registration. There are many ways to do this, most of which involve the use of jigs and forms, but the simplest is to place the succeeding blocks *face down* on the printing paper, then turning over and spooning or running through a press. Colors can be printed one at a time on all the projected prints, or print all the colors on every print as you go along. Experiment for the best method for your print and for your work habits.

The order of printing colors has much to do with the final result. It is best to start with light colors first and work toward the darkest values. However, different greens occur when yellow follows blue, blue follows yellow, the yellow is wet and the blue is dry, the blue is wet and the yellow is dry, both are wet, both are dry, and so on. Here again, experimentation is the key word—and this is where the excitement of discovery lies.

Pablo Picasso's multi-colored prints were produced from a single block by first printing the uncut block in a light color on as many sheets of paper as the edition would contain. If white was to be used, the white areas would be cut out first and the block printed with the second color. He then cut a bit in the block and printed that over the white and first color area with a second color. He then cut some more and printed over the first two, and repeated this process until the last block was only line. This was printed in the darkest color over all the previous printings, and the print was finished. This method needs a lot of forethought as there is no way to go back and correct any misplaced colors. If tone is desired, it can be achieved by using a rasp on parts of the linoleum before printing. If students would like to try it, remind them to keep the shapes extremely simple, and produce a design that doesn't require minute registration.

4

5

51

Steps in the elimination process of linoleum cut printing. You are looking at the inked plates during the various steps in the procedure. First, remove the areas that are to be left white and print the plate with yellow (the lightest ink to be used). Next, remove the areas that are to be left yellow and print in the next color, red. Third, cut away the parts that are to remain red and print the plate in green. Last, cut away everything except what should be printed in black. The final result is a five-color print (below) using white, yellow, red, green and black . . . all printed from a single block. Print by Lois McMillan.

OTHER IDEAS

Additional colors can be made, when oil-based ink is used, by adding oil paint to the ink. Many light value tints can be produced by adding oil paint to white printing ink.

If a line is cut, and you want to eliminate the line, clean out the groove, apply wood dough or plastic wood, and when completely dry, file, carve or sand until even with the surface of the linoleum. Often a linoleum chip or strip can be glued back into place with white glue.

A variation in handling the finished print can introduce color without additional printing. If the block is printed on several different colors of tissue paper, these sheets can be lacquered to a piece of illustration board in innumerable ways. Several can be overlaid for color richness, can be slightly offset when adhered for a feeling of depth, can be torn or cut in various shapes and patterns and adhered, or can simply be glued to a white backing sheet by itself. Care must be taken not to have the color patterns overshadow the print in importance, but with some sensitive handling, this technique can produce beautiful results. Of course, the same handling of materials can be carried out when working with woodcuts, string prints, or many of the other relief printing techniques.

Small areas of second or third color can be added to a print by using stamps made from small bits of linoleum. Some letters, several flowers, gears, or whatever might fit the design can be cut out of scrap linoleum, and mounted on spools or blocks of wood. These can be inked best by rolling out the desired color of ink on a glass plate and pressing the cut design onto the plate and then onto the paper in the appropriate place. Such stamp designs might be used as a repeat background pattern for another design or might be an important second color part of the design itself. But if a repeat pattern is used anyplace in a linoleum cut, it is much quicker to cut one such stamp and print it as many times as needed. Keep these stamps around during the semester, since they might very well be used in another print later on.

Without cutting a new block, a variation in the printing technique can be achieved through another process which works especially well if the block is cut with clean lines. Or a new design may be cut into a new piece of linoleum using finely cut lines in a simple pattern. The plate is then printed with white printer's ink (water soluble only) on white paper. When this has dried, black india ink is brushed onto the print, and when this has dried, the entire design is sprayed or washed with water. The paper absorbs the black ink only at the places that had not been inked with white (the cut out areas of the block) and this produces a black line effect on white paper. Due to various changeable conditions, as the amount of ink and forcefulness of the spray, the resulting prints will vary a bit in their final appearance.

2

1 *Lacquering a print made on tissue paper to a sheet of illustration board. Lacquer is put down first, the tissue is laid over it, and more lacquer is brushed over the paper.*

2 *The top strip is the linoleum block cut with a line and texture design. The second strip is the print pulled in the normal way, by inking and rubbing. The third strip was printed in white water-soluble ink on white paper, with the print then being covered with india ink. When the ink was dry, the entire sheet was washed under a spray which removed the white ink and the india ink that was over it, leaving a black line on the paper. Print by Lois McMillan.*

3 *Facade. Gerald Brommer, linoleum cut, (12 x 18). The single block was printed in black ink on several shades of green tissue paper which were then torn in vertical strips and lacquered to illustration board. Two and three overlappings produce exquisite color combinations and seemingly added detail by multiplication of lines.*

3

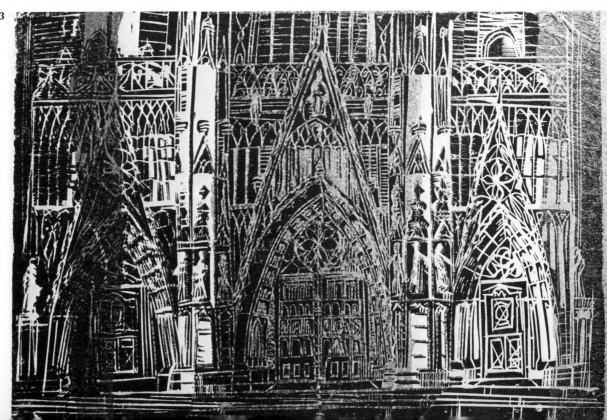

1

2

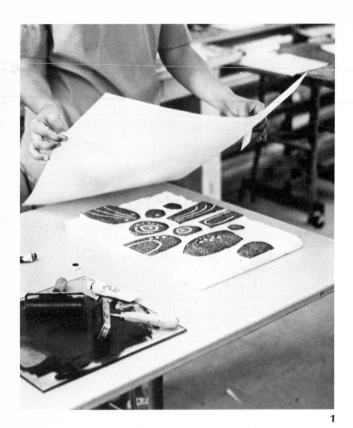

1

3

Additional textures can be added to the linoleum plate by applying white glue or Duco cement to certain areas. These can be textured when wet and when dry will add another element to the surface of the block. Ink the block and print.

If you want to rework an entire area of an unmounted block, say a square inch or more, the offending part can be cut out and a clean piece of linoleum, the same size and shape, can be substituted and recut. The whole block might be glued on a piece of masonite backing or a strip of cloth tape placed across the back of the block to hold the piece in place during printing.

If you want a clean area around the subject, a portrait, for example, the background can be completely cut away with a knife, or tin snips, or if mounted on wood or masonite, sawed away with a coping saw or a band saw.

Keep the printing block clean. Dust and chips of linoleum cause crater-looking formations on the print.

Large flat areas of a second color can easily be made by using a cardboard cutout of the shape required. This can be printed just like a second-color linoleum block. Shapes can be cut with a mat knife and spray-fixed or shellacked before printing. Thin cardboard can be cut out and mounted on another sheet of cardboard or masonite, or thick (1/4-inch) chipboard can be partially cut through, and the cutout shapes "peeled" off, layer by layer, leaving a linoleum cut effect. Spray-fix or shellac, ink and print.

Prints can be made on various background materials; newspaper pages, funny papers, maps, advertisements, tissue paper, scrap wallpaper, colored construction papers or hand-lettered pages. All provide unique and stimulating results.

Group projects can involve printing several blocks side by side; or using many blocks as repeat patterns on huge rolls of butcher paper which can be used to decorate school hallways.

Placing sand on the linoleum, and forcing it into the plate by standing on it, produces a fine-grained background texture. You might have to place a sheet of metal over it so as to force the grains down into the surface. This material (block, sand and metal plate) can also be run through a printing press for even texturing and pressure.

54

4

When ink-stained fingers are likely to produce finger prints on the edge of the printing paper, use folded bits of paper to hold the sheet. Printmakers refer to these practical devices as "paper fingers".

When printing is all done, perhaps the blocks themselves, stained with various inks and with fine luster from the constant rubbing, might make interesting displays. Some students will wish to take the block as well as the print home.

Linoleum cuts can also be combined with other prints—with cardboard prints or with silk-screened prints. They can also be printed on colored paper or printed with colored ink on colored paper.

Remember to make extra prints for student exchange.

1 Using pieces of paper called "paper fingers" to keep inky fingers from spoiling the printing paper. Student is working on a styrofoam print.
2 A single linoleum block printed on three surfaces; first on a magazine page, second on a wood grain print, and third on a tissue collage. Roosevelt High School, Los Angeles.
3 Linoleum cut letters, glued to a scrap of plywood to which a handle has been nailed, can be used for many purposes in other prints.
4 Letters and numbers cut from linoleum scraps and affixed to empty thread spools for easy stamping. These can be used to add interest in other prints, to add textural areas to paintings and prints, or to place words in prints that require them. These were made at Bancroft Junior High School, Los Angeles.
5 Two examples of calendar pages where the illustrative materials were printed in color with linoleum blocks and the letters and numbers were printed in silkscreened colors over them. Bancroft Junior High School.

5

56

THE WOOD CUT

Carving and whittling in wood seems to be one of the needs of mankind—he has been doing it for a long time. By combining this urge with the intricacies of block printing, we have a student-oriented, extremely satisfying printmaking technique—the woodcut.

For centuries the woodcut, the oldest of reproducible art forms, has been close to the action. It spoke for the German Albrecht Dürer as he illustrated the life of Christ for the instruction of the common man. It responded in various colors for the Japanese and told of quiet, serenity, balance and beauty, carrying its message to Europe where it was translated into the idiom of impressionism. It shouted for the Mexicans in the *corrida*, and was sold and sung in the marketplace for all to see and hear. The German expressionists found it an ideal medium for venting their feelings and communicating their fears and desires. And contemporary artists are finding it a useful and responsive addition to their storehouse of techniques. It has been taken out of the realm of the "inexpensive substitute for paintings" and now occupies, along with all types of printmaking, a respected position in the current art scene.

A word is in order, perhaps, concerning the wood engraving and woodcut, and how they differ and are alike. More has been made of the differences than is proper. Traditionally, the woodcut is made on soft or medium hard *plank-grained board* (the way

4

1 Yacht Race. *Lyonel Feininger, woodcut, (5-11/16 x 10¹/₂). The love that the artist had for yacht racing entered into his prints as well as into his oil paintings. Collection, Pasadena Art Museum, California. Bequest, Galka E. Scheyer Blue Four Collection.*

2 Ruins. *Lew Ott, wood engraving, (5 x 8). Notice how the artist has created a sense of various values while working only with pure black and white. Courtesy, Orlando Gallery, Encino, California.*

3 Holy Family. *Albrecht Dürer, woodcut, (15¹/₂ x 11). An extremely fine line quality dominates this master of the German Renaissance, one of the key figures in igniting interest in printmaking. Collection, Pasadena Art Museum, California. Gift of D. E. Wolf.*

4 Hamburg, Harbor and Devil's Bridge. *Karl Schmidt-Rottluff, woodcut, (23³/₄ x 19¹/₄). Strong solid shapes characterize the work of the German expressionists. Collection, Los Angeles County Museum of Art. Graphic Arts Council Fund.*

1

2

wood usually comes—like a diving board), and is cut with a *knife* or *gouge* and produces *black figures on a white ground*. It is usually used for its strong and dynamic contrast of blacks and whites. The wood engraving, on the other hand, is cut into an *end-grain block* of hardwood with *fine burins and gravers* (like those used in metal engraving), and is composed primarily of *white lines on a black background*. It generally is more detailed and can produce more subtle combinations of blacks and whites. For many years, both woodcuts and wood engravings were used for book, magazine and newspaper illustration.

The same differences exist in the media today, but current printmakers tend to disregard them and produce delicate or strong prints with either medium. This is due to the contemporary passion for using unorthodox tools and materials in creating the blocks, and the restrictions of former times on the finished products are thereby abolished. Power tools, flexible shaft drills, screens, nails and a host of personal adaptations can make textures and markings that were impossible to Dürer, Holbein, or Doré. And current printmakers are not reluctant to add materials to the surface of the blocks. Materials like textiles, plastics, metals, cardboard and chips of wood or sand are glued to the printing surfaces. Occasionally these added materials are altered by burning or crushing to produce textures and surfaces that are unbelievably complex.

Because of these innovative and exciting techniques, the traditional differences in types of prints are not eliminated but simply bypassed. Most artists aren't concerned about the pureness of techniques anymore, but the only true values to them are in the finished surfaces and their printed results.

There seems no reason, therefore, to plague ourselves with rigid limits and traditional approaches. The classroom can become an experimental laboratory (which is exactly what an art room should be) that instructs in fundamental approaches, but allows personal freedom of technique and design to dominate the attitudes and therefore the finished work. When approached in this manner, the woodcut can become the most exciting of printmaking techniques, because more personally creative and unorthodox working can take place on the wood block than on any other printmaking surface.

SUBJECT MATTER

Ruggedness and the seemingly crude characteristics of the woodcut have been derided by some uninformed people who have called it an imperfect or folksy art form. The grain of the wood and the broken edges of the printed line make textures an important part of the woodcut. And this is the way it should be. If the design calls for smooth clean edges, and smooth solid black areas, a linoleum print would serve the purpose better.

The woodcut should look like a *wood*cut. There should be evidence of the wood (the grain) and of the struggle between eager student and resisting wood. The textures, the values, the scratches and the patterns should show not only the result of planning and

3

4

1 The Journey. *Lew Ott, wood engraving, (9 x 12). The end grain of the wood was used as a block, and engraving tools were used to incise the sharp design in the wood. Excellent design and interesting variety of textures characterize the artist's work. Courtesy, Orlando Gallery, Encino, California.*

2 Gauguin. *A two-color woodcut (12 x 12) that emphasizes the natural grain of the background block. Baltimore City Schools, Maryland.*

3 Through Patterned Shadows and Shadowy Sounds. *Richard Wiegmann, woodcut, (11½ x 14¼). Excellent use of a variety of textures to simulate foliage. Collection of the author.*

4 Fishing (La Pêche). *Raoul Dufy, woodcut, printed in black. Most people think of Dufy as only a painter, but he was a master of printmaking as this carefully composed woodcut shows. He spent much of his life making blocks for printing fabrics. Collection, Museum of Modern Art, New York.*

5 Old Man. *Two-color woodcut, (11½ x 11½). Lutheran High School, Los Angeles.*

5

1 *Two-color print, making use of the grain in both blocks. Lutheran High School, Los Angeles.*
2 Chicago. *One-color woodcut using the grain of the plank to advantage, to give a feeling of clouds in the sky. Luther High School North, Chicago.*
3 Self-Portrait. *Erich Hechel, woodcut, printed in color. Collection, The Museum of Modern Art, New York.*
4 *Planks of wood, usually pine, come in a variety of widths, each offering its own challenge to the artist.*
5 *Single color block composed of simple shapes, but making use of the unique presence of a large knot. Lutheran High School, Los Angeles.*
6 *The grain of the wood and the struggle of the student with the grain is evident in this woodcut. Lutheran High School, Los Angeles. (15 x 9).*

2

3

design but also the resistance of the wood and the character of the grain. Most contemporary woodcuts give evidence of the fact that they are woodcuts, and not pen and ink drawings. Things can be done with wood that cannot be accomplished with any other material, and it should show. Students tend to be discouraged by accidental chipping, the failure to get a perfect circle, or the inability to recreate the drawn design perfectly. This need not be so, if they understand that we want to retain the grainy, rugged characteristic. That is what gives the woodcut its uniqueness among all art forms.

Subject matter for woodcuts should reflect this ruggedness and simplicity. A delicate child's face would not be as suitable a subject as a rugged fisherman's craggy features; a small delicate animal not as suitable as a charging rhinoceros. Small flowers should give way to rugged trees, and gentle landscapes to rugged mountains or crashing surf. This is not to say that any subject is to be eliminated as a possibility for a woodcut, but when subject matter and the medium are more compatible, more satisfying results will occur. If students are shown the work of the German Expressionists and the handsomely rugged designs of contemporary artists, both representational and non-objective, they will soon see the advantages of selecting subject matter to fit the medium.

MATERIALS TO USE

A block of plank wood, some knives and gouges, a sharpening stone and an idea are all that are needed to begin. Plank grain wood is ordinary lumber cut along or with the grain. It is available in lumber yards all across the country. Length, width, and thickness are up to the student. Generally the scrap bins at lumber yards, cabinet shops, industrial arts classes or family garages will yield plenty of excellent material. If no scrap wood is available, then wood must be purchased from lumber yards, but it is quite reasonable when compared with other art materials. Best for use in the classroom is pine, because of its combination of softness and strength. It often has a grain that is useful, and it is simply pleasurable to work with. It can be bought in any length desired and in finished widths up to about eleven inches. Sometimes planks wider than this are also available. Simply ask for pine one-by-eight or one-by-twelve, but always look to see what kind of grain and knots it has. If you wish to be specific, ask for white pine, yellow pine or Parana pine. All are excellent, with the latter having the closest grain and therefore is best used when fine detail is needed.

If knots come in the wood, try to work them into the design. If this cannot be done, work between the knots or carve them, along with the plank; knots can be quite hard. Other woods like poplar, beech, bass, sycamore, pear and apple, all cut with the grain, are suitable for use, though some might be more expensive in some areas of the country.

Plywood, although it chips and splinters easily, and masonite are coming more into use, especially for the larger prints. Here again, experimentation with the materials will provide some frus-

61

trating and/or exciting experiences. Many contemporary Japanese printmakers are using plywood veneered with silver magnolia, basswood and other woods that were used in plank wood form by the traditional printmakers.

Generally plank wood comes in one-inch dressed thickness, which translates to about ³/₄ of an inch. It is planed smooth, with a bit of grain usually evident, and is ready to work on. If square ends are desired, they should be sawed that way, or at least checked for squareness before beginning work.

Heavily textured wood may be found where it has been exposed to the elements for a long time and the ravages of history have been recorded on it. Look in lumberyard scrap heaps, buildings that are being torn down, beaches after a storm, garages, anyplace that might have a few beat-up pieces of wood that most people would throw away. Don't be afraid to clean them up and use them.

TOOLS NEEDED

Many printmakers rely on a single tool, the knife, to do their cutting. A sharpened knife held firmly at a 45-degree angle to the wood will provide a clean slice. Use as much body power as possible, not relying on the fingers to do all the work. If the block is turned around or the hand and knife are turned over 90 degrees, and another cut is made correctly, a V-shaped slice of wood can be removed. The entire block can be cut in this manner, with gouges being used to remove the large white areas. It is the cleanest way to produce woodcuts, as the knives will not crush some of the wood edges as the gouges might. Students can use X-acto knives, pocket knives or any sharpened tool that feels comfortable in the hand, usually being held like a pencil or a dagger, and drawn toward the body.

All cutting should be done so that each printing area is wider at the bottom of the cut than at the surface. Undercut edges will break off when the block is later burnished in printing, or when other pressure is applied to them.

Some students prefer to use V-shaped and U-shaped gouges from the start, similar to the technique used in producing lino-

1

2

1 Wanted — Jesus Christ. *Woodcut printed in black, but by using varying spaces of black and white, the student was able to create a feeling of value. The print is 21 x 11¹/₂ in size and done in the printmaking class at Concordia Teachers College, Seward, Nebraska.*
2 Sunrise. *Erich Heckel, woodcut, (9³/₄ x 12). Like the paintings of the German expressionists, their woodcuts evoke powerful and imposing images. Collection, Los Angeles County Museum of Art. Gift of Dr. Ernest Schwarz.*
3 Series "Kyoto" No. 34. *Rikio Takahashi, woodcut, (24 x 36). The ten colors of ink employed in this print are multiplied when the overlapping shapes produce extra colors. Courtesy, M. M. Shinno.*
4 *Various brands of woodcutting tools are on the market, but all offer basically the same cutting configurations: V shapes, U shapes and knives. The X-Acto knife in the lower left corner can be used alone, or in combination with other tools in cutting the block.*
5 *The knife can be held firmly, like a pencil, and drawn toward the body.*
6 *Image pulled from a weathered block of wood with the knot missing.*

62

3

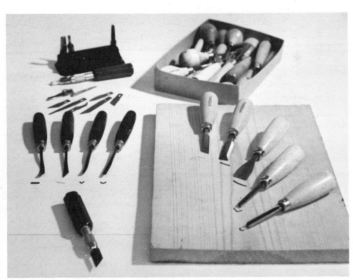

4

6

5

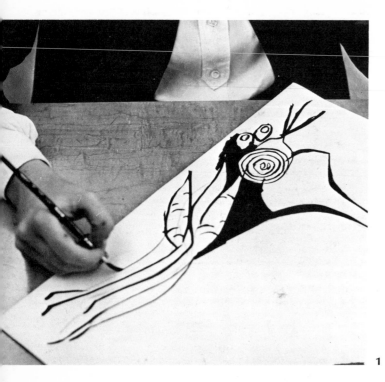

1

2

3

64

4

5

leum cuts. Such tools are available in a variety of sizes and shapes and are very useful in texturing areas, removing large white places, or in cutting the initial lines on the block. The small V-shaped veiner produces a line like two cuts of the traditional knife, but it must be kept very sharp to cut across the grain without crushing it. It is generally much easier to cut *with* the grain of the wood. Because the resistance of the soft and hard parts of the grain varies, care must be taken to keep the non-cutting hand out of the way, since the cutting tools, particularly the gouges, are inclined to skip across the surface of the block at times. A bench hook may be used to hold the block firmly in place while cutting or gouging. It also allows the non-cutting hand to help guide the knife and other tools in the proper directions and keeps the free hand out from in front of the tools.

Gouges are held firmly in the cutting hand, with the palm of the hand producing the force, the fingers only guiding the direction of the cut. If the gouge tip is angled too steeply it will bury itself in the wood, and if held at too shallow an angle, it will skip out of the groove it is cutting.

When cutting cross grain, a slight side to side rocking movement of the gouge should be used to overcome the greater resistance of the hard areas of the grain. Too much straight-ahead pressure will only crush the fibers of the wood.

These are the traditional tools and woods that should be tried and understood before adding the more unorthodox materials to the student toolbox. Contemporary and experimental techniques for texturing and marking the block can be found later in this chapter under *Other Ideas*.

PROCEDURES TO FOLLOW

In beginning the woodcut, as with the linoleum cut, the actual work on the block should be preceded by a few days of thinking and working in a black and white orientation. After becoming used to stating thoughts in single large brush strokes, the student is ready to put his idea onto wood. This can be done by penciling the design directly on the wood and then inking the areas that are to print black, by applying india ink directly on the wood with a brush or by drawing with a felt-tipped marker. If more carefully planned designs are envisioned, they should be done first on paper, then transferred to the block with carbon paper and inked in black. The making of a strong india-inked drawing makes it

1 *Learn to think in black and white by making brush and ink drawings that emphasize strong black shapes.*
2 *After working on paper with the brush, work directly on the plank in the same manner, and when done, begin the cutting.*
3 *Small U-shaped gouges can be used to cut directly into the wood. The design has been drawn on the block with india ink to give a strong indication of the finished woodcut.*
4 *This small (6 x 5) woodcut makes excellent use of direction in the grain of the plank. Lutheran High School, Los Angeles.*
5 The Forest. *Lew Ott, wood engraving, (3¹/₄ x 5). A variety of pattern and spacing of trees keeps this small design interesting and effective. Courtesy, Orlando Gallery, Encino, California.*

1

2

easier to attack the wood and begin to take away the remaining light areas. If you begin cutting with only the pencil lines on the block, you might forget what was intended to be black and what was to be white. The blackened block also gives a more immediate feel of woodcut, as opposed to drawing, and helps to produce a block that feels like a woodcut.

Once the design is inked on the block the cutting can begin, either with a knife or a small V-shaped gouge, removing the areas that are to remain white in the final print. The cut areas need not be too deep, merely enough so that the brayer will not contact them when it rolls across the block. If not deep enough at the time when trial proofs are pulled, the area can always be cut deeper. After doing most of the cutting, a proof should be pulled to check progress. In fact it is a good idea to pull several proofs along the way and keep them as a record of the development of the block. Additional cutting, texturing and proofing should develop into the finished block, ready for printing the final edition.

Although requiring a small space to describe the cutting activity, this is the crux of the entire process. It is here the student encounters reality—the reality of knife and wood and how to make them work together. He must make decisions and be ready for change which is inevitable when chips and splinters create a need for alterations in plans. It is in the cutting that the quality and character of the print are determined, and the confrontation of artist and wood is carried out. It will occupy the longest and most important segment of time in the total woodcut process.

PRINTING THE BLOCK

Basic tools and materials required for printing the block include ink, ink slab, brayer, paper and some kind of pressure to produce the transferred print.

The Inks

Oil based block printing ink or printer's ink, available from a print-shop, are the usual inks used in printing from the wood block. If the ink is too stiff, a miserly drop of varnish, linseed oil, or a bit of ordinary Vaseline will help it run more easily. Don't use too much. Oil paint will also help make the ink more usable, or oil paints themselves can be used as printing ink. These all will use paint thinner or mineral spirits as a solvent and clean-up material.

The water soluble oil, mixed with dry colors, mentioned in the section on linoleum cuts and dealt with in chapter 9 is especially well suited to classroom use on wood blocks. All tools and the block can be cleaned easily with water, and it allows for an infinite variety of colors.

Water soluble inks, used in linoleum printing, tend to dry rapidly on the wood and might provide some problems, although fine prints have been pulled using these inks.

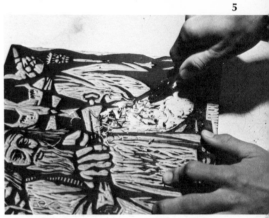

1 Girl. R. Wibr, woodcut, (24 x 12). *Several simple shapes can make a strong impression. Collection, Lois McMillan.*

2 Birth of Wolves. Franz Marc, woodcut, (7 x 9½). *Strong dark shapes swirl around and almost cannot be contained by the edge of the paper. Collection, Pasadena Art Museum, California. Bequest of Galka E. Scheyer Estate.*

3 Gedbedorf Kirche. *Lyonel Feininger, woodcut, (6-7/16 x 8). The artist's strong cubist tendencies are evident in all his woodcuts. Collection, Pasadena Art Museum. California. Bequest, Galka E. Scheyer Estate.*

4 *Soft rubber roller (above) and hard rubber roller with a wood core will both produce excellent results when rolled up properly on the glass plate. The soft brayer will adapt better to surface variations, and is better for inking woodcut blocks.*

5 *The U-shaped gouge is held in this manner, and pushed away from the body. This size is especially useful in cleaning out large areas that are to remain white in the print.*

6 Sky (No. 2). *Tomio Kinoshita, woodcut, (30 x 20). Done in muted colors in the golden brown range, the print has a key block made of black lines which gives the design great strength. Courtesy, M. M. Shinno.*

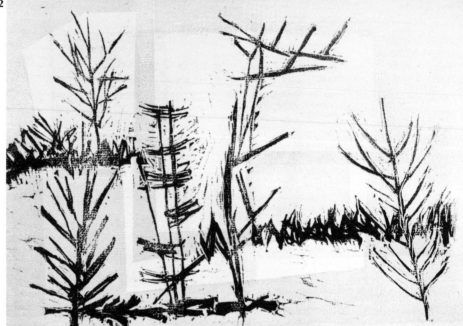

1 *This screeching bird is printed in two colors, and done with two blocks. Lutheran High School, Los Angeles.*

2 Weed Forms. *David Green, color woodcut, (8³/₄ x 12¹/₂). Simple organic forms presented against a second color background. Collection, Pasadena Art Museum, California. Gift of the Pasadena Society of Artists.*

3 Man and Bird in Flight. *Don la Viere Turner, woodcut, (21 x 40). Notice the way the various areas are textured in different ways, yet all seem to belong together. This color print is in the collection of the Pasadena Art Museum, California.*

4 Dawn. *Lew Ott, wood engraving, (3 x 4). Although done on a very small scale, the careful use of pattern and design has produced an almost monumental feeling. Courtesy, Orlando Gallery, Encino, California.*

5 Figure. *Max Weber, color woodcut, (9³/₄ x 6¹/₄). This print is from a book of 33 prints, done in 1918 by the artist, who is much better known for his paintings. Title of the book was Woodcuts and Linoleum Blocks by Max Weber. Collection, The Museum of Modern Art, New York, Abby Aldrich Rockefeller Fund.*

Ink Slab

If marble slabs are available, they make the best ink slabs. They should be large enough so the brayers can be rolled about on them to distribute the ink evenly. Since most classrooms don't have access to marble slabs, sheets of ¼ inch *plate glass* will provide excellent surfaces. Best sizes are about 10 x 10 or 12 x 12 inches. The edges should either be ground smooth when the glass is bought or they should be taped with cloth or masking tapes to prevent accidental cuts. Some friendly glass companies will cut up some of their scrap glass for schools and make them a present of it.

Sheets of metal or formica may also be used as ink slabs, but they should be as flat as possible. Unevenness of the surface will cause the brayer to be inked unevenly.

Brayer

Traditional brayers for woodcuts are made of gelatin and need to be cared for carefully. They should be cleaned with kerosene and hung up to dry, since standing still for a while will produce an obnoxious flat space on the roller. They should not be used with water based inks, as the water will affect the consistency of the roller's surface.

More practical for the classroom are the soft, solid rubber brayers that can stand the hard use students will give them. They come in 4-inch and 6-inch widths, and should be cleaned after use with the proper solvents and allowed to dry. The hard rubber brayers used in linoleum printing can also be used, but the irregular surfaces of the wood sometimes don't receive sufficient ink from them to produce an even print.

Blocks may also be inked with stiff brushes, a sponge, or a leather dabber.

Paper

Initial trial proofs can be pulled on newsprint, bond paper, or some other all-purpose inexpensive paper. Final edition prints should be made on papers that are tough enough to withstand the terrors of a severe spoon rubbing or the stress of a press. There is nothing more frustrating than tearing a paper in the last few strokes of a spooning after ten minutes of careful work.

Rice papers or imitation rice papers are best for the final prints. The Japanese rice and mulberry papers are excellent but they are too expensive for general classroom use. Students might be encouraged to secure a sheet or two for themselves, so they can feel the quality of these papers and their receptiveness of the inks. The smooth side, determined by a bit of rubbing between the fingers, is the better side for printing.

MAX WEBER **5**

6

6 Two Horses. *Takashi Nakayama, woodcut in several colors, (25 x 22½). The artist has combined the feeling of the traditional Japanese woodcut with contemporary forms. Collection, Pasadena Art Museum, California. Gift of the Sustaining Members of the San Marino League.*

Speedball and "3M" both have produced printing papers or "fabrics" which are extremely serviceable. Tableau block printing paper also produces excellent results. All of these have the toughness required and the ability to show ink through during the burnishing process, both important qualities of rice papers. Medium and heavyweight Pelon, obtained at fabric shops is very serviceable and produces excellent prints when the burnishing process is used. All are highly recommended for classroom use.

Bond paper and heavy drawing paper are suitable, and very large prints can be made on heavy butcher paper (the rough side) or brown kraft paper.

Experiment to see which papers give the best results, and which will also suit the feeling of the print. Locally available papers should not be overlooked as possible printing surfaces. Some rough textured papers are very desirable for certain prints but might seem too heavily patterned for other subjects.

The Pressure

Two methods of applying pressure are acceptable in printing the woodcut: one of several burnishing methods and the use of a press.

The burnisher can be the bowl of a metal table or soup spoon held firmly in the hand. If the friction-caused heat is too much to bear, a wooden salad spoon or Japanese rice paddle may be substituted. A smooth stone or the smooth bottom of a glass jar may also be used, as may a metal or bone burnisher or a baren.

The baren is a specially designed wooden-handled tool about four inches in diameter with a slightly convex underside. Its bottom is covered with a teflon material (a substitute for the traditional Japanese oiled bamboo sheath) that allows it to slide easily over the paper.

A solid rubber brayer, if rolled firmly enough over the back of the printing paper, will often produce an adequate result, but the control available with spoon printing is not present.

Some printmakers prefer one of several types of presses, but the burnishing method is still considered better because of the sensitive control it affords the printmaker. If the block is not exactly flat, the press will have a tendency to cause it to crack under pressure.

1

2

3

1 *Rolling up ink from a glass slab, prior to inking the block.*
2 *Tools that exert pressure on the paper to transfer the print from the inked block include a clean brayer, barens, and wooden spoons. A press might also be used.*
3 *Burnishing with a spoon to transfer the image from block to paper.*
4 Landslide. *Edmond Casarella, woodcut, (24¹/₂ x 23¹/₂). Delicate thin lines contrast with strong black and white areas in this print, to produce a vital organic feeling. Collection, Pasadena Art Museum, California.*
5 *Inked woodblock and the resulting print. Don't forget that the image is printed in reverse of the way you worked on the block.*
6 Countries in Spring. *Hodaka Yoshida, woodcut, (20 x 24). A series of fascinating designs, each printed in many colors. The stylized forms make extensive use of geometric shapes. Courtesy of M. M. Shinno.*

4

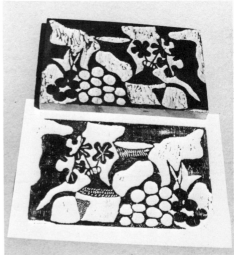

5

6

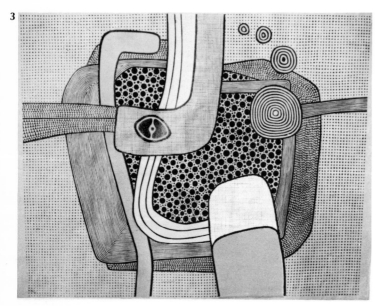

1 *Applying the ink to the block with a brayer. Ink in several directions for best coverage.*

2 *Check several times during the rubbing to make sure the image is sharp and dark enough. If not, reink part of the block and rub some more. Notice the mirror image of the pulled print. If letters or words are to be used in the print, be sure to cut them in reverse, so they will appear correctly oriented in the final print.*

3 *Hanga 66 - 20. Iwata, woodcut on gray paper, (30 x 40). This very large woodcut is printed in six colors, with the final block providing the black line that separates the colors and covers up the registration joinings. Courtesy, M. M. Shinno.*

4

5

Printing the Block

Placing some ink on one end of the glass slab, work it into a more plastic state with a spatula or palette knife, if necessary. Pick some of the ink up on the brayer and roll it across the glass, spreading it in all directions until it is even on the glass and the brayer. A thin film on the brayer is sufficient. Should you need more ink, pick up a bit on the brayer from the source at the edge of the glass slab. Lift up the brayer from time to time in the rolling up process to insure even distribution of the ink on the roller. At its correct consistency, the ink should "crackle" as the brayer rolls over it, but if oil paint is used as the printing ink, this crackling sound will not be present.

Ink the block by rolling the brayer across it in several directions until it is covered. When the block is new, the ink will be inclined to soak into it rather quickly, leaving only a small amount on the surface. This situation will be remedied after several inkings and printings. All that is needed is a thin layer of ink and once this is on the block, repeated rollings of the brayer are wasted motion.

Now place the printing paper, cut a bit larger in all dimensions than the block, on the inked block. Try to get it placed squarely on the block so it will look centered when removed. Burnish with one of the tools described above. Check from time to time, by lifting a corner, to see how dark the ink is printing. If not dark enough, roll a bit more ink on the block and continue burnishing.

When using a rice paper material, the ink will show through the paper to reveal the quality of the print. This saves peeking at the edges to check the ink coverage. If the paper has a tendency to "travel" or move out of position when spooning, it should be weighted down on one end and held in place so the spooning can go on at the other end. When done on one half of the paper, the weight (can of paint, block of wood, etc.) can be shifted to allow for the completion of the burnishing process. The paper can also be tacked in place while working.

Remove the finished print and hang it on the drying rack or place it between blotters to dry. Re-ink the block and pull the second and succeeding prints until the edition is completed. If time limits completion of the edition at one printing, clean the tools and block with the correct solvents, so work is ready to begin again on the following day.

Do not try printing wood blocks by the foot press method described in the chapter on the linoleum cut. Although it is perfectly satisfactory for the resilient linoleum blocks, and would work well on blocks cut from plywood, the plank-grained wood block will undoubtedly crack under the uneven pressure.

When all prints of an edition (say 10 or 20) are pulled, they should be trimmed so about two inches of clean paper surrounds

4 *When finished with the rubbing, pull the print carefully so no smearing of the image takes place.*
5 Lot Cleaning, Los Angeles. *Paul Landacre, woodcut, (12 x 16). Fine details mark the craftsmanship of the artist, who designs his areas and cuts his blocks with extreme care. Collection, Pasadena Art Museum, California. Bequest of Eleanor Bissel.*

the print. They should then be titled, numbered and signed as described in chapter 9.

It would be a good idea, if time permits, to have one copy of each print matted for display, as this is the concluding action on the part of the printmaker. This is also discussed in chapter 9.

MORE THAN ONE COLOR?

The problems and procedures involved with printing multi-color woodcuts have been discussed at length in chapter 2 in connection with linoleum cuts. All the methods described there are applicable to woodcuts as well; however, the textures of the wood will produce richer multicolor areas than will the more evenly surfaced linoleum cuts.

A simple way of getting a second block is to use the reverse side of the main block. Fixing the design, registration and printing are all similar to methods discussed in the previous chapter, except that the same block of wood can be used for two colors—one color on each side.

Gradated color effects can be achieved by rolling the ink heavier on one edge than the other. Two colors can be rolled on one block and overlapped and mixed right on the block, with the brayer, to produce a third color. (Check the illustrations for multicolor techniques and ideas.)

OTHER IDEAS

Today's printmaker is free to employ anything at all to work changes in the surface of his block, to produce the effect he is seeking. Our classroom woodcut projects should likewise allow for some areas of exploration. The average workshop is a treasure

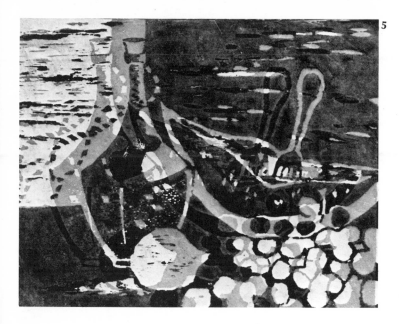

5

6

7

house of useful "tools" for working the surface of the block. Have a board around on which the students may try various tools for the effects they want.

Nails of various sizes, when pounded into the block a bit and removed, will make roundish white areas. Lots of these together can produce a texture, or a few in a row will make a chain-like effect. Several in a dull area will enliven it. The effect is easily seen if pounded into an ink-blackened area.

Electric drills with various bits will either produce neat round

1 Plan carefully to make the most of the two colors you will use. This woodcut is from Lutheran High School, Los Angeles, and is 11½ x 16 in size.
2 The reverse side of the block can be easily used to carve the shapes for a second color.
3 Both sides of the block were used to produce the two-color woodcut. Lutheran High School, Los Angeles.
4 This print was made by collaging tissue paper on a sheet of white paper, and printing the image of the house over it. Roosevelt High School, Los Angeles.
5 Interesting two-color woodcut, produced by simply shifting the second printing of the same block and inking with lighter ink. Lutheran High School, Los Angeles.
6 Rock Forms - Wis. John A. Knudsen, multicolor woodcut created by cutting out the pieces that will be different colors, inking them, placing them back together and printing. Notice the thin white line that separates the colored sections. This is the saw cut. Courtesy of the artist.
7 Storm Breaker. Robert Desota, enamel on wood, (24 x 40). This painting was done by sawing the large board up into pieces, like a giant jigsaw puzzle, painting each part a different color, and assembling it inside a frame. The same technique can be followed in making a multicolored woodcut. Courtesy, Orlando Gallery, Encino, California.
8 Three-color woodcut in tan, brown and black. St. John's Junior High School, Seward, Nebraska.

8

75

1

2

3

1 The Night Sky of Lozenge. *Joichi Hochi, woodcut, (6 x 8). This is a small print by contemporary Japanese standards, but still is done in 6 colors from 6 separate blocks. Courtesy, M. M. Shinno.*
2 Paradox of Youth. *Two-color woodcut, (11½ x 12). Concordia Teachers College, Seward, Nebraska.*
3 *Rich textural surface of a woodcut done in two colors. Nails, electric drills, knives and other tools were used to enrich the surface of the block. This is a detail from a print pulled from a cut plank 56 inches long and 11½ inches wide, done by the author.*
4 Auti te Pape (Women at the River). *Paul Gauguin, woodcut, on end-grain boxwood, printed in color with the help of stencils. The shoulders of the foreground figure have been lowered with sandpaper to produce a rounded appearance. Collection, The Museum of Modern Art, New York. Gift of Abby Aldrich Rockefeller.*

4

holes if drilled straight in, or will make squiggly lines or chew up the surface if run across it at random.

Other power tools, sanders, saws, routers, and grinders can all be employed in experimental fashion to alter the surface of the block.

Cut pieces of screen or wire can be placed on the block, hammered in to make the textures and removed before printing.

Thin pieces of metal can be nailed to the printing surface in places to enliven an otherwise flat and dull area.

Chisels, screwdrivers, hammers, files, rasps, ice picks, screws, nuts and bolts are all implements that will leave telltale footprints as they are pounded or scraped across the surface.

Gravel and sand can be placed on the block, tapped with a mallet or hammer to engrain the surface, and be cleaned out with a stiff brush before printing.

Sandpaper, in varying grades, can be used to scratch, score, texture, or grade the surface and enrich the quality.

To provide a ''gray'' or shaded area of different value, a portion of the block may be lowered by sanding with any desired coarseness of garnet or sandpaper. Paul Gauguin used this method to produce an effect of shading on rounded surfaces.

Substitutes for the wood itself are being used by several of today's printmakers, especially for the large color prints. Masonite panels, plywoods of various types, cardboard, chipboard, mat board and other materials are showing up in increasing numbers in today's prints. Cardboards can be cut with knives, the same as woodcuts, and although not as permanent, they can be used as background shapes or second colors for the key woodcut. When mounted on masonite and shellacked or spray-fixed, they can be quite serviceable.

Small woodcuts or linoleum cuts can be printed over larger woodcuts in repeat patterns or as the center of interest. These can be the same color as the large print or can be a method of introducing a second color into the print. A repeat background of a small block or a group of small blocks can be put down, and the larger key woodcut printed over the resulting pattern.

Materials like paper, wood chips, cardboard, metal, sandpaper, thread, and the like can be glued to the surface of the cut block to enrich it. These should be added only when they will enhance the print or enrich the texture. Care must be taken that the surface does not get too busy, or it will destroy any pleasing effects that might be obtained. Experimentation on a sample block of wood

5

6

7

5 What Sins Do You Confess, My Brother? *This woodcut (18¹/₂ x 9¹/₄) is done in four colors, but two of them are not carved in blocks. The screen is printed in red from a manufactured part, and the small white cross is printed with a wooden stamp. Concordia Teachers College, Seward, Nebraska.*

6 *Various textures can be employed almost like shorthand, to indicate the textural surfaces of the subject. This woodcut was printed in two colors at Lutheran High School, Los Angeles.*

7 *Two-color woodcut (11¹/₂ x 16) that used a simple shape as a second color. The shape was printed by using the back side of the block. Lutheran High School, Los Angeles.*

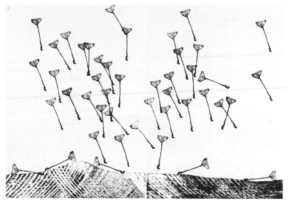

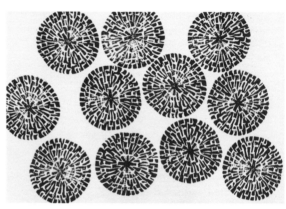

should help determine which textural devices to use. Generally, they are best used in conjunction with some flat black and white areas.

Larger compositions can be produced by using a group of smaller bits of wood carved into various shapes or textures. Stories might be illustrated in this way, or the set of illustrations might produce the story. The book on dandelions is an excellent example of using carved wood stamps to produce a complex set of images.

If your woodcut board is warped, try placing the convex side toward a source of warmth (a stove or the sun). This should dry out that side and restore it to its straightness. But watch the board so it doesn't curl too far in the other direction. If it can't be straightened out in this way, wet it thoroughly and let it dry under heavy pressure on a flat surface.

Finally, when all is completed, take a good look at the stained block itself. Sometimes, after all it has been through, it is worthy of framing as a work of art in itself. Perhaps that is its reward.

And remember to make enough prints so exchanges can be made with other members of the class.

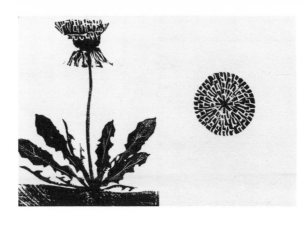

3

1 *Excerpts from the book by Arthur Geisert on the life cycle of the dandelion.*
2 *Small blocks can be carved separately and put together to make a complex print.*
3 *Wooden stamps, carved by printmaker Arthur Geisert, were used in production of a book on the dandelion.*

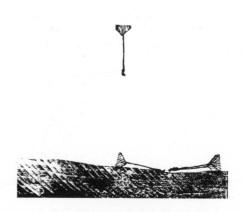

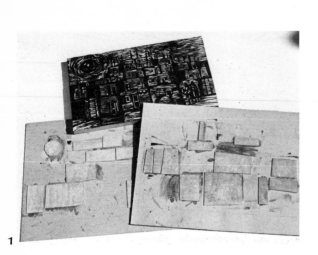

1

2

3

4

5

THE RUSSET
HILLS FALLING
ASLEEP UNDER
THE BIG,
HOT, SUN

OTHER CUT SURFACES

While the woodcut and linoleum cut represent the more classic or traditional approach to relief printmaking involving the cut surface, there are a multiude of new materials and techniques that expand the possibilities of the relief print. And many of them have validity in today's experimental art context. Certainly each person in a class cannot possibly produce every kind of relief print in one or two semesters of work, but when a group of possibilities are outlined, and students can choose one or two ways to go, almost all methods outlined here will be touched on.

Basically, the techniques for preparing the cut relief surface will not vary, nor will the actual printing technique be altered, but the materials will change and each will present its own challenge. The surfaces will all have to be cut or gouged, the resulting cut block will have to be inked and pressure will have to be applied to transfer the print to the paper.

Some materials will be more permanent than others, but all will give an added dimension to the relief print. Let's see what's available and how to proceed. These suggestions might open up new areas as yet unexplored, and if students get caught up in the experimental attitude, they will surely develop some striking and fascinating materials and prints.

1 Two plates made of cardboard provide two background colors for the woodcut of the pueblo at Taos. Cut is by the author.
2 The inked cardboard block is on the right, the resulting print on the left. The unprinted areas were lowered in the cardboard by scoring and peeling.
3 Using a knife to score a design in a sheet of cardboard.
4 Peeling off the scored section for a cardboard print. The unpeeled part will remain a bit higher in relief than the peeled part, and will therefore produce a printable design.
5 Experimental print made by cutting and pulling off the thin layer of a piece of corrugated cardboard. Such trial prints might lead to more refined and finished products.
6 Cut cardboard letters to print the words from a poem. The illustration was done with a linoleum block. Overall size of the finished combination print is about 16 x 12. Lutheran High School, Los Angeles.

6

81

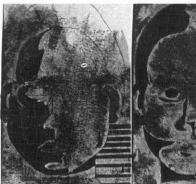

1 *Four separate cardboard plates used in producing a four-color cardboard print. Courtesy, Lois McMillan.*
2 *Cutting letters from thin cardboard and adhering them to a backing sheet of 1/8 inch chipboard.*
3 *Burnishing a cardboard cut using letters.*
4 *Another dual-material print, the illustration done in linoleum and the lettering cut from cardboard. Lutheran High School, Los Angeles.*
5 *Inking a design on a plaster of paris disc with a felt marker.*

CARDBOARD BLOCKS

Cardboard can be used like a woodcut, except that the quality of the material will serve the printing of large flat areas better than parts with much detail. If used for simple shapes or for a background color and shape for woodcuts or linoleum prints, it is ideal.

Any cardboard between an eighth and a quarter of an inch thick will serve as the block. The drawing can be done right on it and can then be darkened with india ink or a magic marker. The remaining light areas can then be cut around with a sharp mat knife or an X-acto knife. These areas that are not to print are lowered by peeling off layers of the cardboard. Simply insert a knife point under one of the cut corners and lift up and peel off.

When the cut is complete, shellac or spray-fix the surface to harden and protect it. If this is not done, subsequent treatment with the moist printing ink will cause the surface to deteriorate.

The texture of the cardboards may vary: pebbled mat board, irregular chipboard, textured boards of various types. Even corrugated board is worth a try, as the ribs will be exposed when cut and can provide some excellent impressions.

Soft edges can be produced by tearing rather than cutting the shapes.

If letters or numerals are needed, they can easily be cut from lightweight cardboard, mat board, or tagboard and either glued to another sheet of cardboard to make words, or can be inked and printed at random, individually or in combination.

Small cut cardboard shapes can be used to produce added color effects in woodcuts or linoleum prints. A dress pattern of flowers or geometric shapes can be printed with several small repeated cardboard cutouts rather than cutting the entire pattern free from the original woodblock. Similarly, repeat patterns in backgrounds or wallpaper can be done in this way. The cardboard can be glued to the end of a block of wood and stamped in the desired locations on the print.

The cardboard can be cut into an infinite variety of shapes, attached with strong glue to a backing board and made ready for printing by spray-fixing or shellacking.

When used in combinations with fabric, sandpaper, textured papers and plastics, surfaces can be obtained that will print in ways impossible for the more conventional woodcut to duplicate. Experiment with combinations of materials.

More cardboard ideas are presented in chapter 7 which deals with built-up relief surfaces for printing.

PLASTER BLOCK

The major difference between the plaster block and previously discussed relief print methods is that the student printmaker must first make the block—it does not come prepared for him. This can be done by sifting plaster into a bowl of water and mixing with the hand until a thick creamy consistency is reached. This is then poured into a mold about one-inch deep (made of cardboard,

5

1

2

3

4

1 Plaster block print which was inked with water-soluble ink, burnished with a wooden spoon and printed on a sheet of typing paper.

2 Cutting and chipping white areas from the plaster design with a wood-cutting gouge.

3 A plaster block cut used as a repeat pattern, printed over a brushed tempera background. Revere Junior High School, Los Angeles.

4 The plaster block at the left was formed in an aluminum pie tin, and then carved. The resulting print, on the right, was printed in black over a tissue collage. The block is 8 inches in diameter. Revere Junior High School, Los Angeles.

5 Plaster block printed over a brushed tempera base. Shapes must remain simple and bold because of the character of the carving material. Revere Junior High School, Los Angeles.

6 Cutting a design in a styrofoam sheet. The areas to be left raised are outlined with a felt marker, while the negative area is removed by cutting with an X-acto knife.

5

wood, masonite, plasticine, or a combination of these) and allowed to dry and set overnight. Aluminum pie tins also make excellent round forms for the plaster. When hard, it is ready to cut.

Because of the character of the material, fine details should be avoided and large and vigorous shapes should be developed with emphasis on shape and line. Designs can be scratched, cut or dug into the surface of the plaster with nails, knives, screws, pieces of heavy wire, or linoleum or wood cutting tools. Loose plaster should be brushed away.

Plaster blocks should be sealed with shellac before printing to overcome the tendency to absorb most of the printing ink into the porous surface. A coating of ink, allowed to dry, also may act as a sealer on the block.

When inked, the paper should be placed down on the block and rolled out with a brayer or rubbed with a wooden spoon. Burnishing should be done carefully because the edges of the plaster cuts might break under heavy spoon rubbing. If a baren is available, the burnishing can be done with it rather easily.

STYROFOAM AND GEN-A-LITE

Flat blocks of styrofoam an inch or more in thickness are best to work with and can be cut from larger blocks or sheets available at most craft shops, florist supply stores or variety stores. Shapes, rectangular or irregular, can be cut with a knife, single edge razor blade or electric styro cutter knife.

Tools to cut or mark the surface are easy to find. Knives or razor blades will make clean cuts while any tools, even a pencil or a finger nail, will make printable marks. The softness of the cutting surface is a bit tricky to handle, since anything will mark it and therefore will print. A pencil is a good tool to score the surface, producing fine lines. But this very softness will allow the quick preparation of the block for printing. Objects like jar lids, tools, nails, etc. can merely be pressed into the surface to make marks. These indentations, combined with sharply cut lines or an interestingly shaped block, can provide some excellent prints. The surface of the styrofoam itself will provide an interesting bubbly texture when printed.

Designs may also be burned into the styrofoam surface with an electric woodburning pencil.

The design or subject matter should be extremely simple, since complex detail is not possible due to the softness of the material. Care should be exercised when working with the block so areas that are to print will not be crushed or indented by the eager printmaker.

When the simple design is cut or scratched or pressed into the surface, the block can be inked with a soft rubber brayer, rolled firmly over the surface. Liquid tempera paint may also be brushed onto the block with a bristle brush and used instead of printing ink.

The block is placed face down on the printing paper, which may be lying on a pad of newspaper. It might be advantageous to lay a flat board or sheet of plywood on top of the block to distribute the pressure evenly and prevent crushing parts of the block. Rub-

6

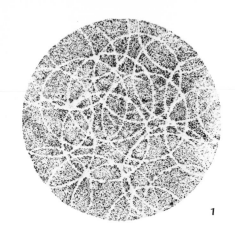

1

2

bing firmly with the hand or a baren will also produce satisfactory results.

Styrofoam might also be used, because of its textural qualities, as a second color block or background block for a linoleum or woodcut. It can stand alone as a print, or small areas of other prints can be enhanced by printing repeat designs with small styrofoam blocks.

If prints do not show sufficient detail, try using dampened paper, and print by placing a dry sheet of paper over it and rubbing.

Gen-a-lite is a bit more resilient than styrofoam but should be handled in the same way. The large blocks can be cut into more practical sizes and shapes with a knife, single edge razor blade or an electric styro cutter.

ERASERS

Plain and unglamorous rubber, art gum, or soap erasers, the kind often left on the art room floor, make excellent printing tools. They can be left in their squarish original form or can be carved with a razor blade or knife into myriad shapes.

Pressing the cut eraser onto an ink pad will gather sufficient ink to produce a print when stamped on paper. Various colored ink pads can be used to produce multicolored effects, or making a pad of dampened newspapers and tempera paint will provide even more colors.

Repeat patterns, either carefully structured or printed at random, are most easily carried out with the eraser print. Experiment with a variety of hand pressures, or with printing again and again until the eraser is almost dry, or pressing more firmly on one side of the eraser than the other. All will give variety and interest to the quality of the print.

Again, these eraser prints can be used to liven woodcuts or linoleum cuts with added form and/or color. They also can be used to create wrapping paper, greeting cards and the like. When used with textile printing ink, they can decorate the edges of scarves, handkerchiefs or skirts. The possibilities seem almost limitless.

OTHER IDEAS

A wide variety of other materials, both natural and cut, can be used to print. They may be used in repeat patterns as finished

1 *Styrofoam print made from a round piece of material in which a jar lid was pressed to produce the design.*
2 *Inked styrofoam block and the resulting print. The more the block will be printed, the darker and more solid the printed image will become. Part of the block has been carved with an X-acto knife, while other marks were made with a pencil.*
3 *The design is drawn on the flat of the eraser and the negative space cut away with a knife.*
4 *Cut eraser print used in a repeat manner to create movement.*
5 *Printing eraser prints in various patterns, using an inked pad as a source of color.*
6 *Eraser print using a stylized letter of the alphabet, and repeated to develop movement. Printed on oatmeal paper. Lutheran High School, Los Angeles.*

3

4

5

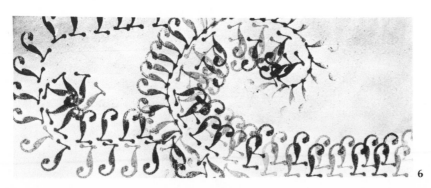

6

products, or they can be printed in conjunction with other prints as indicated on previous pages.

Potatoes, turnips and carrots can be cut to simple shapes and printed by applying tempera paints with a brush and pressing on paper. The cut forms can also pick up color from a flat metal or glass sheet on which tempera paint or colored ink has been brushed. If the "block" isn't too juicy, it can also pick up ink from a regular ink pad.

Other vegetables and fruits can be cut and either printed directly or allowed to shrivel a bit and then printed. Best "ink" to use with these is tempera paint or colored drawing inks, brushed on and pressed down to print. Think of vegetables and fruits with interesting organic interior patterns; citrus, cucumber, tomato, green pepper, cabbage, and so on.

The Japanese produce beautiful fish prints by inking the side of a fish and printing it on fine rice paper. Care must be taken in applying just the right amount of ink so fine details of the complex texture are not lost.

Modeling clay and wax can be used like the plaster prints described before. Prepare the plate, scratch press or cut the design, ink and print. Experiment with other such materials that might be printed in the same manner.

Leaves of all types can be inked with a brayer or brush and pressed to the paper with a clean soft rubber brayer to make the print. Such prints can be repeated to make a pattern or used as a background for another block.

Sponges, crumpled paper, cloth fabric and materials with "ready made relief" can produce an infinite variety of background textures for other prints. Or, by printing them over themselves with other colors, a richly patterned and textured surface can be developed that is intriguing in itself.

More experimental printmaking techniques can be found in chapter 7 which deals with built-up surfaces for relief printing.

The patterns of individual inventiveness are easily observed when students are exposed to a variety of ideas and allowed to develop their own innovations. It is in meeting the challenges of new techniques and materials that the students grow in their understandings and attitudes toward the materials of art. Experimental printmaking provides such avenues of direction.

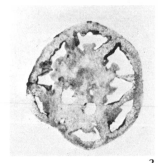

1 *Orange print, using tempera for ink.*
2 *Tomato print, using tempera for ink.*
3 *Repeat design using a carved potato section. The variations in value of the printed parts comes from continued printing without re-inking the potato.*
4 *Cut potato print, using light value tempera for ink and printing on darker surface.*
5 *Bell pepper print, with the vegetable cut and allowed to shrink a bit before printing.*
6 *Clay print, 4 x 6 in size, printed from slab of clay in which the student had drawn with his finger. The clay was "inked" with tempera paint, and the print rubbed with the hand. Revere Junior High School, Los Angeles.*
7, 8 *Various leaf prints, made by inking the leaves and pressing them onto a sheet of printing paper. The delicate lines in some leaves are more evident in the prints than in the leaves themselves.*

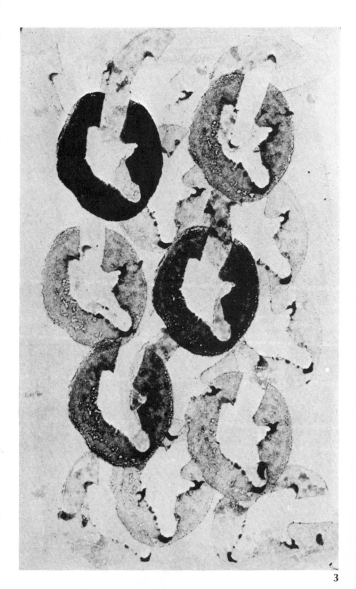

3

4

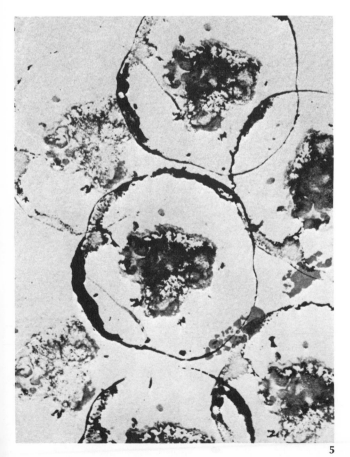

5

7

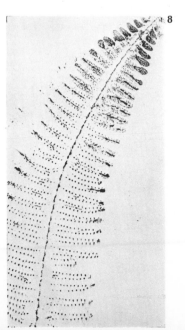

8

1

2

3

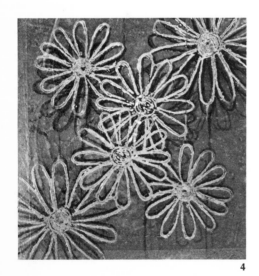

4

5

STRING PRINTS

When speaking of relief prints, the countless materials and techniques can be broken down into two major types: one which removes part of the surface and one which builds up the surface to be printed. Both use the raised areas that receive the ink to make the printed marks on the paper, but each arrives at this relief in a different manner. The first part of this book deals with surfaces that are cut into and have the negative areas removed. The chapters that follow (5–7) will explore the possibilities of printing from built-up surfaces.

Combining a few of the simplest materials available, string printing is an excellent technique for introducing relief printing from built-up surfaces. While employing primarily the use of line, it is a method of working that can indicate to students the range of possibilities inherent in printing of this nature. When first working with the medium, it can be used alone, while later it may be used in conjunction with other materials in several other techniques.

MATERIALS AND TOOLS

String, in any of its many forms, is needed. Although plain cotton string works very well, everything from thread to clothesline rope has been tried. Generally speaking, the string used in preparing the printing plate should be of the same thickness, since hard rubber brayers will not be able to touch all surfaces if varying thicknesses are used. If a soft rubber brayer is used, it will be able

1, 3 *String prints printed on bond paper from the inked plate.*
2 *Singing bird is printed in light ink on dark tissue paper and laminated to a white backing. Lutheran High School, Los Angeles.*
4 *One flower design, printed at random in several colors on several colors of tissue paper and laminated together with lacquer.*
5 *String print, done on various colors of tissue paper which were cut up and reassembled on illustration board. The same three fish appear three times in the finished work. Lutheran High School, Los Angeles.*
6 *Design taken from German cathedral makes excellent use of single line technique. The string was inked and paper pressed against it for reproduction. Size: 24 by 12. Lutheran High School, Los Angeles.*

91

6

to ink various levels of relief and the consistency of the string need not be so carefully watched.

Strings of various hardness, texture, and thickness can be brought into the classroom for use. They can be bought in cones or balls or spools, or students can bring odds and ends from home. It is best to try a few types before beginning the preparation of the plate.

The plate itself can be either a piece of heavy chipboard, cardboard, matboard or a piece of masonite, cut to the correct size.

Glue of some type, usually polyvinyl acetate (Borden's, Elmer's, Wilhold, or the like) is used, although any glue, cement or paste might be successful. The plate receives some rough treatment in printing and the stronger the bond between string and plate, the better.

No special tools are needed, with a single edged razor blade and a toothpick taking care of the requirements.

1

PROCEDURE TO FOLLOW

Cut a sheet of cardboard to a convenient size, with about 12 by 18 inches being comfortable in most cases. The heavier the string, the larger the plate should be. Select an idea from the sketchbook or some other source and work out a simple line drawing of it. Contour drawings make ideal subjects for string prints, and one taken from the sketchbook should be satisfactory. Place the drawing in pencil or pen on the cardboard plate, or draw directly from a student model onto the plate.

Two methods of adhering the string can be followed. A bead of glue can be laid down over the line with a plastic squeeze bottle, and the length of string placed down on top of the glue and patted and directed into place with a toothpick or the tip of a finger. Another method is to brush an area with glue, including the background area, and place the string on the penciled line while the glue is still wet.

However it is done, the string must be stuck on the board in some way. Excessive lengths can be cut from the glued string on the board with a razor blade. Where two lines cross, it is good to cut one rather than have a bulge which will show up on the print as an extra dark area. (Perhaps this would be interesting in some prints.)

The plate can be proofed from time to time, simply by rubbing the side of a crayon over the sheet of paper laid on top of the

2

1 *Contour drawings from sketchbooks make excellent subjects for string prints.*
2 *Draw in line first on the cardboard backing.*
3 *String print, made by rolling the plate with a soft brayer, placing the paper on the plate and rubbing. Thin hard string was used which has no texture of its own, and produces a very sharp image. Size is 20 by 12, done at Lutheran High School, Los Angeles.*
4 *Put down a bead of glue from a squeeze bottle on the penciled line.*
5 *Put the piece of string down on the bead of glue.*
6 *Using scissors to correctly position the string in a critical area.*

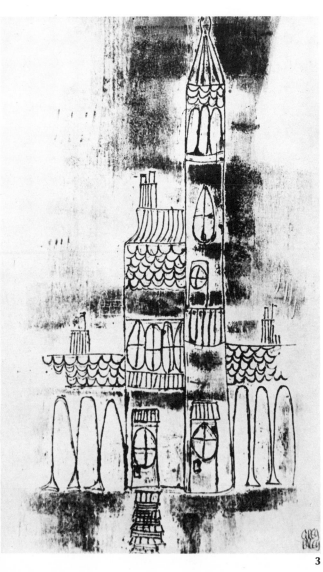

3

4

5

6

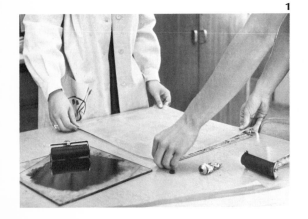

1

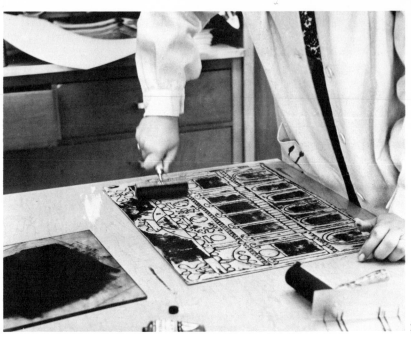

2

3

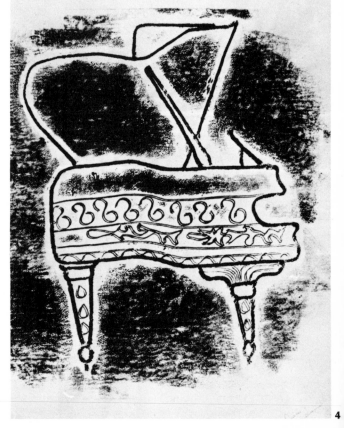

1 *Help might be needed in correctly positioning a sheet of tissue paper on the large inked block.*

2 *Using a hard rubber brayer to ink the string block.*

3 *Using a clean brayer to apply pressure to the tissue paper sheet. A finger might do the job as well.*

4 *Print made by using a soft brayer to ink the string printing plate. When the background receives some ink also, the resulting print has a halo effect around the string lines. Several thicknesses of string were used in this print, heavy for outline and light for details. Lutheran High School, Los Angeles.*

5 *The soft lines of a string print, inked by rolling the inked brayer over the back of the paper, can be very effective.*

6 *Rolling a semi-inked brayer over the back of a sheet of paper placed on the string print plate. Notice the soft, fuzzy effect of the line. Too much ink on the brayer will blotch the paper and make it unusable.*

7 *Rubbing a sheet of bond paper to transfer the print from the inked plate.*

94

4

plate. A nearly dry brayer can also be used for this purpose, rolling it over the *back* of the paper placed on the plate.

Solid areas, if desired, can be built up of coils of string or sections cut to length and glued side by side.

Finer and harder string will produce clear sharp lines, while softer cotton strings will provide a different feeling. Choose the one best suited to the subject matter, or mix them up. It is a good idea to test the strings on a scrap piece of cardboard before beginning the big plate. Continue adding string and proofing until the plate is finished.

PRINTING

The raised surface of the plate can be printed in two ways. The string can be inked with water soluble or oil based ink by running a soft or hard rubber brayer over the surface. The soft brayer will deposit ink on spaces between the lines. If this is objectionable, the harder brayer should be used. Experiment.

Printing paper, probably bond paper, tissue paper, rice paper, or drawing paper, is then laid on the inked plate. Pressure can be applied by running a clean brayer over the back of the paper or rubbing with the flat of the hand, spooning, or placing on the floor, putting a pad of newspaper or a magazine over it, and stepping on it.

This method of printing will provide a fairly clean, mirror-image, the reverse of the plate, and probably will show the fine texture of the string. Another method will produce an image that will duplicate the plate in its directional orientation. Place a sheet of paper on an uninked plate, and holding the paper firmly in place, or taping it so it cannot travel, run an inked brayer over the back of the paper. This will produce a soft and fuzzy line that often has the quality of lithograph or a soft pencil drawing.

It is best, in this technique, to roll the fully inked brayer on a sheet of newspaper or scrap paper before applying it to the back of the printing paper. A fully loaded roller will not recognize the subtle relief variations through the paper and will blotch the print. A nearly empty brayer is best. Experience will dictate the quantity of ink and the best method to use.

The paper used in this method of printing should be quite thin, with a bond or tissue paper working quite well. Experiment. If the paper is too heavy, the roller will not "read" the string impression through it and will provide the printmaker with a more or less solid inked sheet.

This technique may be expanded to involve the printing of two successive images, in two colors perhaps, slightly off register, to suddenly double the number of lines used. One printing may be made lighter, simply by using a drier brayer.

OTHER IDEAS

It might be interesting, with some designs, to print the direct and the mirror images on the same sheet of paper, flipping the sheet over and printing the second image over the first.

5

6

95

7

1

2

3

4

5

6

7

8

Color can be introduced by using colored ink or colored tissue or construction paper. Perhaps inking with several colors without moving the print would be interesting.

Movement studies are simple to produce by moving the paper successively in one direction and using the same brayer without re-inking it.

Prints can be made on tissue paper and adhered alone or in various combinations to white bristol board or illustration board. This can be done with lacquer, which makes the tissue even more transparent than it already is. See illustrations for several ideas on this technique.

Save the plates when finished with printing. They may be used later and printed as a collagraph, or they can be left alone if they are richly stained with printing inks. They may even be painted on at a later time, with the string providing a fascinating relief under caseins, acrylics or oils.

Only the size of the cardboard and time will limit the size of the plate and the resulting print. When working very large, be sure that large enough paper is available to make the print.

1 *Lacquering the tissue printed pieces to illustration board.*
2 *When rolling the inked brayer over the back of the paper, the image will duplicate the plate, not providing a mirror image. The plate is on the right, the print on the left.*
3 *The print is receiving its second printing, over the back of the paper, and slightly off register to double the lines on the facade of this cathedral.*
4 *Applying lacquer over the top of the tissue paper to finish the laminating process.*
5 *Rolling a partially inked brayer over the back of the paper two times, slightly off register, produces a feeling of minute detail. This print is about 30 by 20 in size. Lutheran High School, Los Angeles.*
6 *Image printed in dark and light ink on tissue papers, with the light lines being laminated over the dark ones to produce a fascinating shadow effect. Lutheran High School, Los Angeles.*
7 *Rolling an inked brayer over the back of the paper to produce one of several successive images in a motion study problem.*
8 *Don't throw away the string printing plates when you are done printing. This plate was later painted with casein, the string providing interesting relief patterns. Lutheran High School, Los Angeles.*

3 Man Sitting

1 Studio Scene. Glen Alps, collagraph, (25½ x 40). A variety of richly textured areas is one of the characteristics of this printmaking medium. Collection, Pasadena Art Museum, California.
2 Locomotive built of cardboard and string provides active subject matter for this collagraph. Lutheran High School, Los Angeles.
3 Seated Man is composed of glue, tissue paper, string, cardboard and burlap, and is 18 by 12 inches in size. Lutheran High School, Los Angeles.
4 Magnificent textural surface was created by using juniper leaves and the bark of several trees. Though difficult to run through the press, the embossed and inked surface of the paper was richly detailed with texture. Size is 18 by 14. Lutheran High School, Los Angeles.

98

COLLAGRAPH

Although professional printmakers have used raised metal surfaces for some years, the collagraph is a fairly recent addition to school-adapted graphic techniques. A sort of in-between method of working, the collagraph combines the effects of collaging and the results of printmaking. It makes use of the effects and qualities of intaglio processes as well as the application and techniques of relief printing. And when handled sensitively, the collagraph can produce exceptional results, rich in coloring and texture and vital with a true printmaking appearance.

The background of the collagraph lies in the tactile and visual stimulation of the collage, a twentieth century contribution to art from the creative and prolific talents of Pablo Picasso and George Braque. Running his hand over a well-prepared collage, a printmaker can easily recognize that an inked brayer applied to that surface will produce a print.

While a collage is prepared by gluing colored paper, cardboard, string or other materials to a ground in order to produce a pleasing design, a collagraph uses the same technique to produce a print. But where the collage requires use of colored materials and often the addition of paint to complete the work, the collagraph needs no color in the preparation—that is provided by the ink when the print is pulled.

MATERIALS TO USE

The collagraph as a medium is extremely versatile, allowing for a fantastic range of materials in its preparation. These are glued to a backing plate, inked and run through a press to produce the finished print.

The plate itself can be either heavy (1/8–3/16 inch) chipboard or 1/8 to 1/4 inch masonite. Lighter materials can be used, but the stress of the press and the general abuse which the plate takes in preparation and printing requires a heavy, substantial backing.

Materials are glued to the surface with a strong glue, and should be flattened down on the plate. These materials may include the

4

following, although this is not a complete list by any means: string, thin wood strips, toothpicks, thread, cardboards of various textures and thicknesses, flat pieces of metal, wire, screen, pieces of linoleum, scraps of tire tubes, fabrics of various weaves, paper, plastics, plant life of various types (usually leaves and flowers), feathers, crumpled and flattened tissue paper, sand, tree bark, wood veneers, etc., etc., ad infinitum. These materials can be glued on as they are or can be altered by cutting, scraping, gouging or scoring. A mere razor blade scoring line will show up on the print as a thin dark or light line, depending on the inking process. Many ready-made flat objects of metal, plastic or cardboard may be incorporated into the collage. Washers, gaskets, and other cutout materials can be used.

Armed with a box full of such material, a bottle of glue and an idea for a print design, the printmaker is ready to go to work.

PROCEDURE TO FOLLOW

Sketching an idea (from life, still life, sketchbook or imagination) onto the cardboard or masonite backing plate is the beginning of this exciting adventure into printmaking. Once this is simply stated in line, the building up process begins. Choosing materials that suit the subject, or that simply are esthetically pleasing at the time, the student adds piece by piece to his collage. String and thread will serve as line, as will cuts made by knives or razor blades. Flat areas can be produced with cardboards, papers or flat metal sheets adhered to the surface. If a piece of plywood or a plank is used as the backing, items can be attached with nails and the nailheads become part of the design.

Ready-made flat forms can be incorporated. Textures can be provided with crumpled tissue paper, cloth fabrics, textured paper or by scratching, gouging or otherwise marking up the surface of either the backing plate or the added cardboard pieces.

Glue itself, when hardened, will add another material and before it dries it can be scratched or drawn in for more textures. Any liquid metal, gesso, modeling paste, or plastic can be added to supply shapes or a material for texturing. Check the illustrations for ways these materials can be used.

PRINTING

When the collaged plate is completed, it should be shellacked for protection and permanence, and allowed to dry. It is then ready for inking and the press. Several inking procedures are possible, depending on whether the class has access to a press or not.

The simplest inking procedure is to load a soft rubber brayer with ink and roll it across the plate, working it in several directions to distribute as much ink as possible to all the raised surfaces. A soft paper, one of the rice papers or imitation rice papers (Tableau, 3M Printmakers Fabric or Speedball Printing Papers) are best for this. Be sure to hold the paper firmly while printing so it does not travel. The back of the paper should then be rubbed to provide

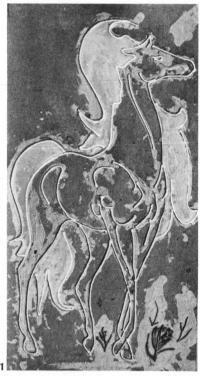

1

2

3

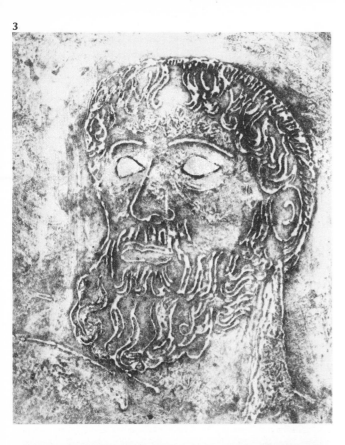

1 *A collagraph plate, prior to inking. The horse is made of string and glue, with the large white areas being built up of P.V.A. These areas will provide an embossed feeling to the final print. Lutheran High School, Los Angeles.*

2 *String, white glue and feathers went into the building up of this collagraph surface. Background shows evidence of the rubbing that took place in inking the plate. Lutheran High School, Los Angeles.*

3 *Collagraph of a Roman sculptured head was done with glue and string, and printed with gray oil paint. Size is 16 by 14, done at Lutheran High School, Los Angeles.*

4 *Rearing Horse. The plate is on the left, the print on the right. Notice the way the glue areas print and the line that the string makes. The finely detailed textural areas are made of crumpled tissue paper. Lutheran High School, Los Angeles.*

5 *Cutting cardboard pieces and gluing them to a board on which the preliminary design has been drawn with pencil.*

6 *Gluing bits of paper to a collagraph plate, prior to inking and printing.*

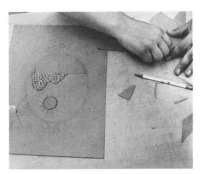

5   **6**

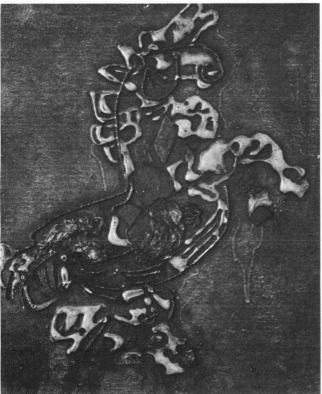

4

101

1

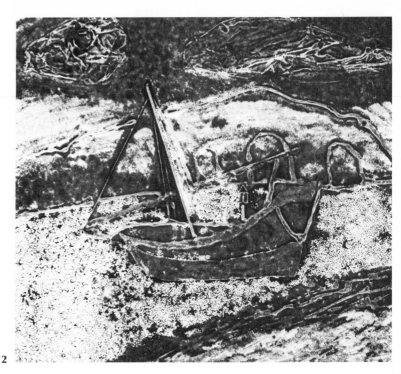

2

3

4

1 *The head of David was remodeled of white glue and string, the former giving a sculptural quality to the finished embossed print. Size is 14 by 12.*
2 *Sparkling texture in the water was accomplished by gluing sand to the plate.*
3 *The intricate textures of this print were made by simply gluing crumpled tissue paper to the cardboard plate, then inking, rubbing and printing in a press. The forms are almost crystalline.*
4 *The decorative tree was made completely of white glue on cardboard, then rubbed with green-black oil paint and printed in the press. It is 16 by 13 in size, done at Lutheran High School, Los Angeles, as were all other prints on this page.*
5 Island in the Sun. *Print made from plate composed entirely of cutout cardboard parts.*
6 *Inking the collagraph plate with a bit of cloth on which oil paint has been placed.*
7 *On the bed of the plate is placed a clean sheet of newsprint, the collagraph plate, the printing paper which has been dampened and the quarter inch felt blanket.*

the pressure. This can be done with the hand, a soft rubber brayer, or by pressing with a pad of cloth, to pick up as many of the subtleties of the printing surface as possible. The print should then be hung up or stacked between blotting paper sheets to dry.

The second method of printing, and one which provides the most accurate transfer of the plate's surface to the paper, combines some of the intaglio and relief process features. Oil paints are used as the printing ink, and they are rubbed onto the plate with a bit of cloth—rubbed in all directions until the plate is covered. The rubbing can continue with the original inking cloth or with a clean cloth, picking up some color from areas which should be lighter and burnishing other areas until the richness of the plate is evident. Various application and rubbing techniques should be tried until the most satisfactory for each print is discovered. Don't rub off too much ink!

5

On top of this inked and rubbed plate lay a sheet of *dampened* paper, the paper a bit larger than the plate. It should be heavy printing paper, like that used by intaglio printers, or very heavy drawing paper. Experiment with dampened papers; some heavy papers not normally used for drawing or printmaking give excellent results.

Paper can be dampened by holding it under the water faucet, wetting both sides completely, and placing it between sheets of blotting paper for a while. It can also be dampened by preparing a dampened pad of newspaper, wetting the stack thoroughly with a large soft brush about every 3 or 4 sheets. Sandwich the dry sheets of printing paper into this pad every couple of sheets and place a weighted plywood or masonite panel on top of it. After half an hour or so, the paper is ready to use. Insufficient wetting will cause irregular inking of the print.

6

The inked plate with the dampened paper on top of it should be placed on the bed of the press. One or two felts should be placed over the paper (again experiment to see what works best for you) and the whole sandwich run through the press. A clean sheet of newsprint should be placed under the printing plate on the bed of the press to keep the print itself clean and free from picking up stray ink from the bed.

The resulting print should be hung up to dry, or placed flat between sheets of dry blotting paper, or tacked by all four corners to a wall or bulletin board. Another method, used by intaglio printers, is to tape the print with gummed paper tape to a sheet of plywood or an old drawing board. As the paper dries, it shrinks and is stretched flat smooth. It then needs to be cut from the plywood with a mat knife or razor blade.

This second printing method will provide the students with yet another printing technique and will afford them the opportunity of working in a way not previously encountered. It is stimulating and fascinating and produces excellent results.

Hands are cleaned with paint thinner, but the plates need not be cleaned, as they will have very little ink left on them if the pressure has been sufficient to transfer most of it to the paper. The ink-stained surface of the plate, if several colors of paint have

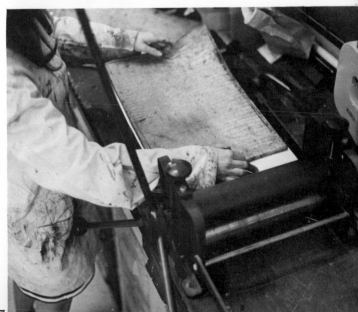

1

2

been used, is rich and lustrous, and can be kept as a finished piece of work itself.

When the edition is printed and dry, it should be checked and the best ones selected for numbering and signing.

OTHER IDEAS

When using the press method of printing, try to keep all the initial plate thicknesses the same (like 1/4 inch chipboard) as this makes adjusting the pressure of the press to each plate unnecessary. Minor adjustments might be needed for plates that are exceptionally built up.

Oil colors for the press method should be kept in the earth color range: burnt sienna, burnt umber and Mars black work very well. These can be used alone, in rubbed combinations or succeeding each other, since the second printing will tend to pull a little color from the previous run.

Students will find their own variations and procedures after pulling a few prints. Encourage experimentation with color, rubbing, paper dampening, pressure, etc.

Prints can be blind embossed, if no ink is put on the plate and simply dampened paper is used. This will produce a non-colored print of the plate, but the strong relief in some of these can produce interesting results.

Because of the messy rubbing procedure, paper that is clean should be handled with "paper fingers", small rectangular scraps of newsprint folded over the edge of the paper to keep unwanted finger prints from cluttering up the clean border of the print.

The size of the bed of the press will limit the size of the print. Since it is advisable to have a small edge of clean paper around the print, the original plate on which the collage is done should be at least an inch narrower than the width of the press bed.

If string prints were done prior to attempting collagraphs, they can be shellacked, inked in the manner described above, and run through the press.

Remember to produce enough prints to exchange with classmates.

3

4

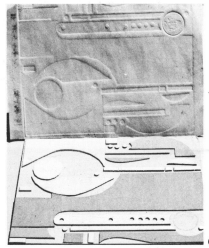

5

6

8

7

1 Rolling the printing sandwich through the press provides the pressure to transfer the image from plate to paper. The felt allows for the embossing of the paper.
2 Checking the plate after printing. The plate is on the bottom, the print is being pulled to check coverage. Following this printing, the plate can be re-inked and printed again.
3 Bits of material, string and screen went into the plate which produced this 18 by 12 print. Lutheran High School, Los Angeles, California.
4 A jolly little turtle was made of string and glue. Lutheran High School, Los Angeles.
5 Inked plate was built up of string, glue and actual leaves and twigs. Size is 10 by 14.
6 A collagraph plate, printed without application of ink, produced a blind embossed image. Roosevelt High School, Los Angeles.
7 Clothes for these two printed people were made of actual materials of various textures. Material and string were glued to the plate, which was shellacked, and then inked and printed. Lutheran High School, Los Angeles.
8 The ink-stained collagraph plate itself can be a handsome piece of art. Notice the light reflecting off the textural surfaces of this plate which is made of cardboard, papers of various weights, tissue paper, sand, leaves and glue. Work is by the author.

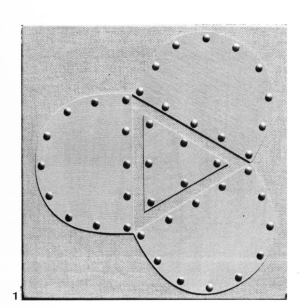

1

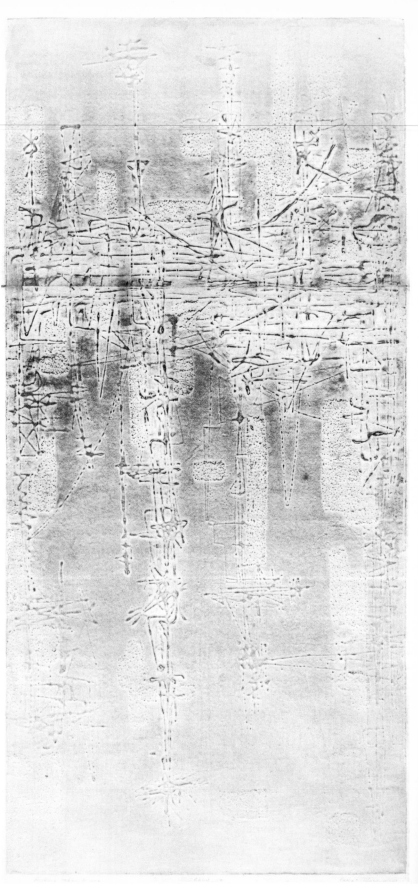

2   3

OTHER BUILT-UP SURFACES

If experimentation is a key word in today's art scene, the area of built-up relief surfaces for printmaking certainly is in keeping with this trend. Besides the techniques listed in the two previous chapters, there are actually countless methods left to explore. With current technology daily increasing the items we have to work with, we should keep a receptive mind and an eager eye open for new and challenging materials. All of these materials require but one method of working: that of the built-up surface that is inked and printed. The materials used are vehicles toward perceptive development: the printmaking activity, regardless of the materials used, is the mode of creative expression.

A number of suggestions will be dealt with in this chapter, certainly in no particular order or arrangement. They are only offered to whet the appetite for further exploration. If these techniques intrigue you, keep an eye peeled for articles in *School Art* and *Arts and Activities* for the constant stream of new suggestions which avid art teachers offer their colleagues.

4

1 *An untitled work by Edie Danieli, composed of burlap, metal sheets and tacks on a piece of wood, is not made to be a printing surface. But if a brayer were rolled across it and it were run through a press, it would produce a fascinating print. Courtesy, Orlando Gallery, Encino, California.*
2 *Strips of metal, nailed to a plank, were inked and printed.*
3 Across the River. *Boris Margo, cellocut print, (52 x 25). Marvelously intricate lines weave a subtle design in this large print. Similar work might be done with white glue or Duco cement on a cardboard surface. Collection, Los Angeles County Museum of Art. Gift of Otis Art Associates.*
4 Departure. *Edmond Casarella, paper relief cut, (30 x 22). Wonderful flowing movements were created by the printmaker simply using pieces of cut paper to print the design. Collection, Pasadena Art Museum, California.*

DUCO CEMENT

Perhaps one of the simplest of all printmaking experiences involves the use of Duco or airplane cement, or similar material, on cardboard. Make a simple line drawing on a sheet of cardboard, matboard or scrap of wood, plywood or masonite. Squeeze a line of Duco cement directly from the tube onto the line and let it dry. The drying might take several hours.

The cement raises a surface above the backing sheet which may be inked with a roller and printed. A soft roller will also ink the background and produce a "halo" effect around all the glue areas. A hard brayer will ink only the surface of the Duco line, and will print much like the string print. If the Duco is laid on a wood surface, the use of a soft brayer might allow for a grained wood background to show behind the glue line.

When the block is inked, lay the paper down on it and roll a clean brayer over the back to transfer the ink to the paper. Rubbing by hand may also produce a print, as will running the plate and paper through a press. Placing the plate and paper face down on a pad of newspapers on the floor, the printmaker can step on it and allow his body weight to provide the pressure.

Variations of the technique include putting the Duco on a glass sheet and rolling the ink over it. However, if large classes are working, the wood block or cardboard plates are more inexpensive and more easily stored.

As in string printing, the impression may also be printed by putting a piece of paper on the uninked plate and rolling an inked but semi-dry hard rubber brayer over the sheet.

Another variation involves the use of rubber cement instead of the Duco. Brush the rubber cement on a piece of glass, allow it to dry, run an inked soft rubber brayer over it, apply paper, and press with the palm of the hand or a clean brayer. Beautiful textural surface can be obtained with this method.

FELT BLOCK PRINTS

If scraps of felt from old hats or other projects are around the art room, they will provide the raw materials for another kind of relief print. The pieces of felt can be cut with scissors or a razor blade into simple shapes and glued with white glue to a piece of cardboard, masonite or wood. Because of the need for simplicity, shapes should be bold and vigorous, and emphasis should be on the space relationships of the various parts.

When the design is complete, it can be inked over with a brayer (experiment with kinds of ink) or covered with tempera paint and a brush, and stamped on the printing paper. If the blocks are small they can be pressed down by hand, but if larger, might require placing them on the floor and standing on them to exert even pressure. Spooning also produces satisfactory results.

The felt will at first have a tendency to absorb much of the ink or paint, and a few trial prints on scratch paper or newspaper sheets will help determine the amount of ink and pressure to use to get the desired result.

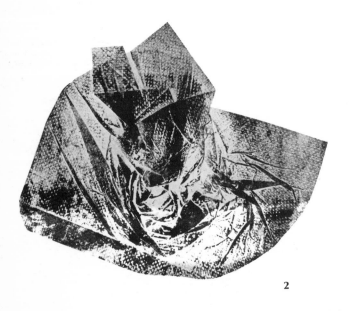

1

2

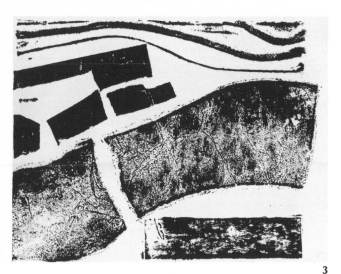

3

1 *Print made by forming rubber cement on a glass plate, inking and printing on a sheet of paper towel. Eight by four inches in size, the print is from Revere Junior High School, Los Angeles.*
2 *The texture of the paper towel is evident, but the lines made by the crumpled sections provide movement and excitement in the design. The towel was glued to a piece of cardboard, inked and run through a press.*
3 *An experimental design, using cardboard, felt and various strings. Titled "Pathways", the 8 x 10 print is from Concordia Teachers College, Seward, Nebraska.*
4 *Designed area, 12 by 16 in size, printed from block made of burlap and felt glued to cardboard plate. Lutheran High School, Los Angeles.*

4

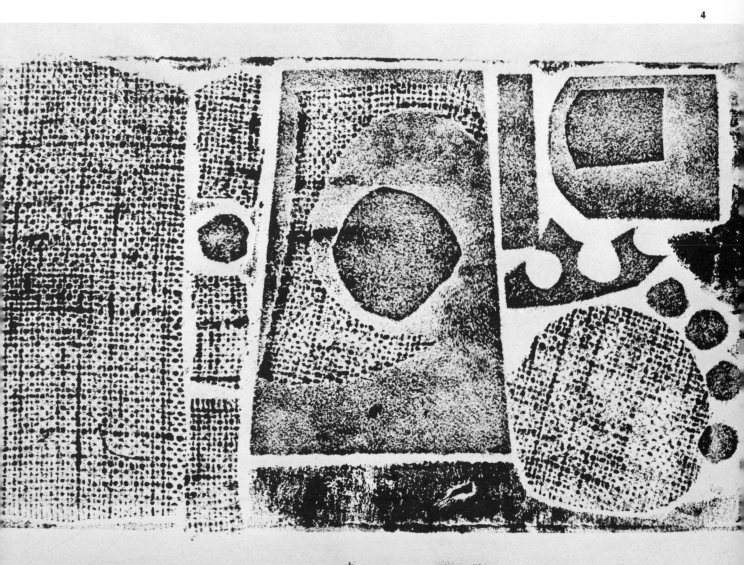

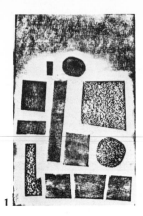

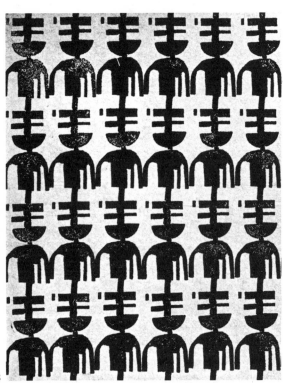

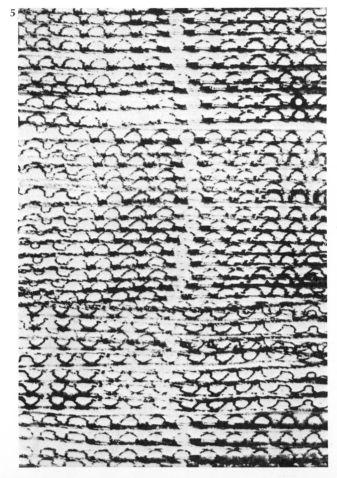

1 *Simple experimental design using various cardboards as the printing elements.*
2 *Letters cut from tagboard and glued to thin cardboard which has been trimmed to avoid printing too much background material.*
3 *Overall pattern printed from a block made of inner tube material. This was used as a portfolio cover, and made by Lois McMillan.*
4 *Collagraph printed from a plate which was made entirely of cut pieces of cardboard. Size is 12 x 16, done at Lutheran High School, Los Angeles.*
5 *Overall pattern made by printing the edge of a piece of corrugated cardboard.*
6 *In the center is the printing plate, made of string, inner tube rubber and buttons. At the left is the resulting print, to the right, the print made on a tempera background. Work by Lois McMillan.*
7 *Abstraction. Walter Dexel, woodcut, (9¹/₂ x 6). The bold and simple shapes of this woodcut would lend themselves to printing in other materials, like cardboard, rubber inner tubing, or paper. Collection, Pasadena Art Museum, California. Bequest of Galka E. Scheyer Estate.*

110

Backgrounds for these prints might include a brayer rolled color or a sponge printed texture—or the felt blocks themselves might be a second or background color for another print.

NEOPRENE AND RUBBER TUBE BLOCKS

Other materials that are easy to cut and therefore easy to work with are to be found in a number of non-art-store places. An excellent example is the spongy black material that skindivers and surfers use for their wet suits. It is a 1/4 inch neoprene material and can be easily cut with scissors or razor blades into simple shapes. The material can be found in scrap barrels of aquatic supply stores.

The cutout pieces can be arranged on a wood block or cardboard or masonite sheets, and glued in place with white glue. When dry, the design may be stamped on paper after inking with conventional ink and a brayer or coating with tempera paint and a brush.

Repeat designs and patterns of simple, bold shapes are conveniently printed in this medium, while designs requiring small detailing are to be avoided.

A change in amount of pressure applied to each side of the block will provide interesting variations in the resulting color intensity. Experiment with pressure, application of ink to the block and the "carving" of the neoprene material itself.

A discarded automobile tire tube can be cut and used in a similar way. Arrange the parts of the design carefully before gluing to the plate surface.

CARDBOARD PRINTS

As indicated in chapter 4, various cardboards are readily adaptable to making relief prints in several ways. The cardboard can be cut, scored, and/or peeled to produce prints following the traditional linoleum cut method. Or it can be cut into shapes and adhered to a cardboard sheet to produce a printing plate.

Lightweight and medium weight cardboard is best suited for this, as the cut edges are clean and sharp. The design should be sketched on a heavy sheet of cardboard or masonite. Pieces of cardboard in various shapes and sizes can be cut and glued to the surface with white glue. The areas cut and mounted will be the positive printed shapes, because the loaded brayer is rolled across the block, depositing ink on all the raised areas.

If pebbled mat board or other textured boards are used, they will add to the surface richness of the finished product. All the relief methods of printing and overprinting can be used to develop the final product.

Cut out in this manner, cardboard printing plates will provide excellent second- or third-color plates for other printing media, such as the woodcut or linoleum cut, or they can be used as excellent patterns or designs themselves. Stressing the importance of shape and spatial relationships, cardboard prints can be used in many design oriented problems.

6

7

111

Shapes made of cardboard and glued to a backing sheet can be used to emboss textures or shapes on a previously printed paper. A press must be used to apply the pressure to a dampened paper.

TAGBOARD AND HEAVY PAPER

Oaktag and heavy papers can also be used in printmaking, but the technique has to vary to print these materials carefully. While cardboards are thick enough to keep the relief of the added sections separated from the backing sheet in brayer inking, oaktag is not thick enough and must be handled a bit differently. It will not be glued to a backing surface.

Since there will be no sheet to hold the cutout pieces together, the design will have to be set up like a stencil—with all parts connected. This will provide an impetus for stylization and simplification. The design should be either outlined on the oaktag and then inked in, or inked directly with a brush or a magic marker. If the area to print is made black, the student will obtain an immediate visualization of his print.

The design should then be cut out with a sharp knife, razor blade or pair of scissors, taking care to keep all the parts to be printed connected together.

The cutout design can be laid on a sheet of scrap paper and inked. Placing it next on a clean sheet of paper—inked side up—press the printing paper down on top of it. Roll a clean brayer over it to print, or rub with a spoon.

The print can be made on clean printing paper, newspaper, magazine advertisements, or any of a multitude of backgrounds. Several colors on different "blocks" can produce intricate designs when overprinting each other.

LIQUID MATERIALS THAT HARDEN

Not all built-up relief surfaces need to be cut shapes that are glued to a panel, but some very interesting textures and designs can be worked in materials that can be spread on the plate. Such liquidy and brushable materials include Sculpmetal, gesso, modeling paste, white glue, cement, and casting resins. All of these take considerable experimentation to understand the proper time involved in drying and how long it remains workable. But if samples are made on small blocks, this should be determined after a few trials.

All methods of working involve the same procedure, but the drying time involved and resulting prints will vary a bit. Prints done in this way may be used as background for other prints or may stand on their own merits as completed works.

Backing plates should be substantial so that warping can be kept to a minimum. Masonite, plywood, partical board and very heavy cardboards are the best. The material (Sculpmetal, liquid solder, gesso, white glue, or whatever is used) can be smeared on with a palette knife or spatula and spread over the entire surface. When the consistency is right (and this will vary with the materials), begin to work in it with a stick, brush, nail, pencil, pieces of cardboard of various widths, etc., developing a relief design. Con-

112

1

2

3

4

1 Overlapping design using moving people cut from tagboard, glued and inked. Lutheran High School, Los Angeles.

2 Dual print, involving a linoleum cut at the top and a cardboard cut to produce the letters at the bottom. Line is from a poem and the total print is 24 by 10 in size. Lutheran High School, Los Angeles.

3 Because of their stencil-like appearance, these two linoleum cuts might easily have been made as a paper print. Both 12 x 20 in size, these cuts are from Los Angeles High School.

4 The surface for this print was made by brushing gesso on a heavy sheet of cardboard, 14 by 18 in size. When dry and hard, the block was inked with a soft rubber brayer and printed in a press. Lutheran High School, Los Angeles.

5 An elephant is enmeshed in the leaves of this jungle which was made by distributing liquid metal (Sculpmetal) on a sheet of heavy cardboard. Some of the material was drawn in with a pencil, some was trailed off the end of a stick, and other parts were textured with various tools. The dried plate was inked with a soft rubber brayer, and the plate and paper were sent through the press. Lutheran High School, Los Angeles.

5

113

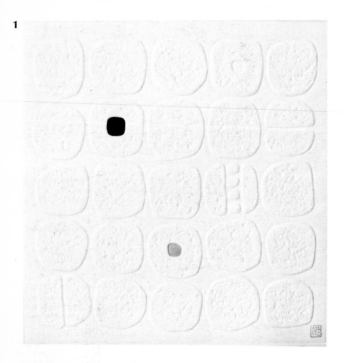

tinue working until the design is finished. If desired, other materials like sand can be added to the liquid before it dries, increasing its textural possibilities. Dripping or trailing some of the material can produce marvelous spidery patterns. Various of the above materials can also be worked over each other in combinations that will further alter the finished print.

A second method of applying the liquid-that-will-turn-hard is to brush or spread it on with a spatula and create the design as the material is put down, perhaps leaving some areas uncovered.

If necessary, when dry, the surface can be cut into with a mat knife or it can be sanded or steelwooled or scored with other tools to create special effects.

When the texturally rich plates are dry (usually overnight), they can be inked with a soft roller or the ink can be rubbed on with a cloth as in printing the collagraph. Pressure in either case can be applied by burnishing with a spoon, rolling a soft rubber brayer over the paper or running the plate and a piece of dampened paper through a press. If this latter method is used, be sure there are felts on top of the paper so the full embossing can take place along with the transfer of ink from plate to paper. Different effects are achieved from the same block with each printing method used.

After the printing is finished, the plates themselves can be burnished with fine steel wool, and in most cases the ink-stained relief surfaces will provide very exciting textures. Many are worthy of keeping or framing.

OTHER IDEAS

Among other materials that can be cut and/or adhered to blocks for printing are the following:

Adhesive Foam, a thick, white, moleskin type material found in the "Dr. Scholl's" section of the local drug store. It is adhesive backed and can be cut or trimmed to shape and applied to the block with its own adhesive backing.

Plastic weatherstripping cord, which often contains a self-adhesive, can be stuck to a cardboard plate which has had a design penciled on it. When the design is finished it can be inked with a brayer and printed by placing the paper on it and rolling a clean brayer over the back of it. The line produced by this cord is much heavier than the normal string print, and the subject matter should be bold and simple to take advantage of this.

Burlap and other open weave fabrics can provide interesting second color shapes or textural background colors for other prints. Glue the material in place, ink and print by burnishing or standing on the block to exert pressure.

Cut pieces of metal like tin cans, aluminum plate, or old zinc offset printing plates can be nailed to a piece of 1 by 12 pine with wire brads with heads. Nails and metal alike become part of the design. Ink in several ways to see which best suits your design. The plate can be inked with a brayer and burnished or put through the press; or it can be inked by rubbing oil paint on with a cloth and running the board and dampened paper through a press—as in the collagraph technique. The metal can even be scratched in a drypoint intaglio method incorporating several printmaking techniques in a single print.

✳ It should be easily discernible that the materials available in combination with several inking and printing techniques can provide the serious printmaker with years of experimentation. The art room in school should partake a bit in this excitement of discovery. Have students gather unorthodox materials and see what ideas they can come up with. Relief printmaking is no longer just linoleum cuts and woodcuts, although it is important to work with them. There is no end to the possibilities.

1 Cell. 8 - 1. *Haku Maki, woodcut, (16 x 16). The rounded squares with the textured surfaces were embossed in the paper using cement forms on the woodblock. Colors were added with stencils. Courtesy, M. M. Shinno.*
2 *An etching plate, printed by the relief method. In the normal intaglio printing, the white lines would appear black. This print is actually a negative of the traditional printing process. Plate is by the author.*
3 *Scrap of burlap, printed with water-soluble ink applied with soft rubber brayer.*
4 *Pieces of a tin can were cut up and nailed to a board to provide the block for this experimental print. Lutheran High School, Los Angeles.*

4

1

2

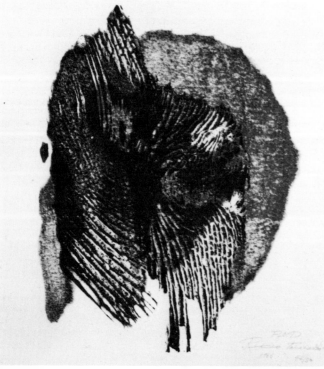

4

3

EXPERIMENTAL PRINTS

In recent years, relief printmakers have turned more and more from the conventional cut surfaces of wood and linoleum and have found a new vitality in a wide range of new materials, formed shapes or found objects. While countless pieces of printable subject matter are all around us, it takes a sensitive artist to put several of them together to produce a cohesive design and successful print.

This does not lessen the need for the student printmaker to become aware of these techniques. Perhaps the only value he will receive from materials printed in such experimental form will be the pleasure and excitement of seeing the results themselves, or the experience of working in the experimental media.

For ten or more years, Michael Rothenstein of England has led a professional and student task force in searching out new methods of working with relief prints. The far-reaching results of his research will undoubtedly affect relief printing for years to come. But printmakers in the United States and all over the world are engaged in the search for new forms that are reproducible in relief printing. The contemporary Japanese printmakers have done fascinating things with the surfaces of the wood and have produced multicolored prints that are astounding in concept and technique.

This chapter will provide a very brief insight into the new world of relief printing.

5

1 *End grain of a Douglas fir 4 x 4, printed twice.*
2 *The end of a log can produce several interesting textures, including the growth rings of the tree, the saw cuts, and the stress lines produced in the drying process.*
3 Flood. *Rikio Takahashi, woodcut, (10 x 7). Small bits of wood, inked and printed over each other to produce delicate image. Courtesy, M. M. Shinno.*
4 *The delicate graining in a sheet of ordinary plywood.*
5 *Simple design printed from metal washer and scrap of wood. Overall size is 8 by 4 inches.*

117

WOOD GRAINS

Richly textured planks of wood, ravaged by storms and the beating sun, can provide an excellent experience in printmaking. Such fragments of nature, untouched by the knife blade or gouge, can supply visual images that may stand on their own merit, or be used in combination with other materials to produce design effects. To make student artists more directly aware of their environment and the multiplicity of materials available for surface enrichment in printmaking, the finding and printing of wood fragments is a vital experience.

Weathered and textured plank wood, saw cut cross-grained slices, slivered veneers, climate-exposed plywood, worm-ridden hardwood logs, charred and shattered stakes and planks may all be used to create delicate patterned or ruggedly monolithic prints. They can form a study in sensitivity, because the handling, inking and printing of such pieces is not easy, but when done successfully is extremely rewarding. Such blocks, planks, stakes, sheets and pieces of wood should be gathered and brought into the art room. Several days can be spent in making print studies from them so students may become perceptive to the innate qualities of wood.

The surface of the delicately grained wood should be inked with a stiff printing ink, since softer ink will flow into small cracks and obliterate nature's design. Black oil based ink, regular printing ink, or water soluble inks will provide excellent results.

A soft brayer can be used best to place ink only on the raised portions of the block or sheet. Use only a thin layer of ink so the image, sometimes very shallow, will not be covered and drowned in the inking. Soft ink and/or a soft brayer can be used on heavily textured materials of greater relief. The older and rougher surfaces can be inked with old brayers, the kind that are about ready to be thrown away.

Paper used for such printing can include smooth bond paper for delicate textures of wood with softer rice paper-like material being used for the coarser textures. Very coarse textures might require dampened paper.

The paper should be placed on the inked wood and burnished with a wooden spoon. During spooning, the paper may have a tendency to travel—move around under the constant rubbing—and pick up a double or triple image. If this might happen, place a weight of some kind on the paper to hold it in place, have a friend hold it in place for you, or thumbtack it to the block or a backing board. Very rough blocks might require the edge of the spoon, in burnishing, as well as the rounded bowl. Fingertips or a pad of rags might be needed in some extreme cases to get the paper down into the textures—if this is desirable.

Thin papers might require a second sheet over them during the spoon-burnishing to prevent tearing.

Because of the irregularity of the surfaces, printing such textures on a press is extremely difficult but might be attempted to judge the result in each case. Experiment with various inking and print-

1

2

3

4

5

1 *The marks left by the growing larvae of the bark beetle produce a fascinating surface, worthy of the printmaker's attention. These prints were produced by inking the side of some logs from which the bark had been stripped and burnishing with a wooden spoon. The prints were done on rice paper which is easier to control on an irregular surface than harder papers.*

2 Birth Mark. *Hiroyuki Tajima, woodcut, (26 x 20). Marvelously rich surface textures are evident in this exciting print. The viewer certainly wonders how the artist scored the surface of his block to obtain this final result. Courtesy, M. M. Shinno.*

3 *The woodpile is a fascinating place to search for wood textures. Every piece of wood produces its own unique print.*

4 Shapes, *a woodcut (10 x 8) printed from cutout bits of wood. Notice that textures run in different directions with each separate piece. Concordia Teachers College, Seward, Nebraska.*

5 *Scrap of Douglas fir, two by four, inked and printed. Surface is not weathered, but still provides sufficient texture for printing.*

1 *Experimental print employing all sides of the metal formed part shown at the top.*
2 *Group of ordinary materials ready to be printed in experimental fashion, to learn the possibilities of printing such found objects.*
3 *Reprinting a small metal piece can produce interesting overall movement pattern. Size is 8¹/₂ x 11.*
4 *The image of the inked top of a radiator grille.*
5 *An inked bit of aluminum window screen produced this image.*
6 *A single large (2 inch) metal washer, printed six times.*
7 *The bottom of a decorative decanter inked with a soft rubber roller. The clean circles were printed by pressing down on a solid surface, the circles with the star-like designs in the center were pressed down on a padded surface.*
8 *Print made from a rounded beach stone, to study its texture. Stone was inked and rolled on the paper.*
9 *Experimental cluster prints made by stamping the ends of the two felt tipped markers.*
10 *Flower design stamped with the lid of the ink tube and a piece of cardboard, printed on edge to make the lines.*

1

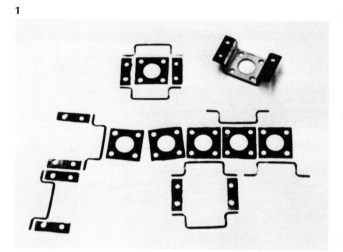

2

3

5

6

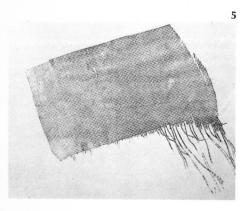

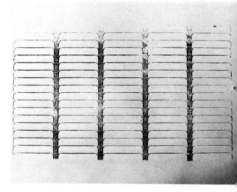

ing methods, as each piece of wood demands individual consideration.

If soft parts of the wood intrude or clutter up the fine linear quality of the design, a steel brush, either hand or motor driven variety, will easily remove them, but be careful to always work *with* the grain, not across it.

Wood surfaces might also be altered by burning with a blow torch, or pouring alcohol on part of the surface and burning it. Charred parts might be printed or removed with a steel brush or rotary steel brush attached to a motor driven shaft.

8

9

ROCK AND STONE

Found chunks of slate, granite, marble, quartz or a myriad of other rocks can be inked and printed. If the surfaces are relatively flat, the paper may be put down on the stone and printed. But if rounded rocks are to be recorded in print, they can be inked, pressed down and rolled around on the printing paper which has been placed on a thick pad of newspaper.

Though not as responsive to printmaking as wood fragments, rocks can still provide some visually beautiful surfaces in the search to record our environment in ink.

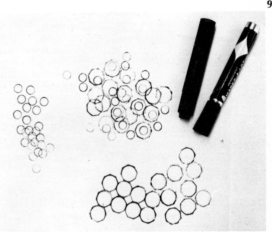

USING MAN-MADE MATERIALS

Today's plethora of manufactured materials offers the experimental printmaker a never-ending challenge. Metal and plastic in particular are available in countless materials and forms, and if a printmaker is attempting to record his environment in ink, these materials are worthy of experimentation. Using manufactured items to produce prints is one way of making use of the technology of today, and mating that technology and art.

Using such man-made materials falls into three categories: prints obtained from unaltered objects (gear wheels, cast metal, glass or plastic parts, etc.); prints received from manufactured items that have been altered accidentally (crushed, flattened, shattered, eroded, etc.); and prints that are pulled from objects that are altered purposely (hammered, flattened, bent, broken, etc.) to produce a desired effect. All three sources of materials are worthy of a bit of time in experimentation, and a few of the ideas will be outlined here.

10

USING UNALTERED MANUFACTURED OBJECTS

Any manufactured surface that will accept ink can be printed, and some, naturally, are more interesting and useful than others. They may be printed and enjoyed for their intrinsic values, or they may be experimented with for possible inclusion in later conglomerate and complex prints.

Students can bring in a list of printable materials and items almost immeasurable in length, but here are a few that will provide a start: gears, electric motor parts, clockworks, all types of

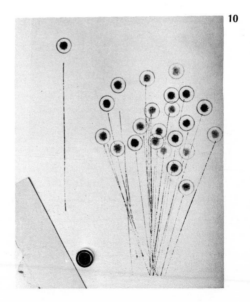

machine parts, wire fencing and screening, the tooled masonite backboard from a radio, gaskets, all sorts of stamped metal or plastic parts, tools, various cast, die cut, extruded or injection molded pieces of metal, plastic, glass or fiber material.

These can be inked with an oil or water based ink, tempera paint, or regular printing ink and a brayer. Experimentation will determine the best methods of inking and printing, since each material offers its own challenge.

USING ALTERED MANUFACTURED OBJECTS

Manufactured objects of metal or fiber can often be found in altered condition: crushed, eroded, or flattened. This change from the original shape was not planned, but an accidental happening, and can be recorded in printing ink.

Tin cans flattened by tires or trains; various metal objects crushed in the junk yard; rusted, corroded and worn-out metal plates of steel, iron, tin, lead or copper; weathered roofing paper; crackled and deteriorating painted surfaces; crumpled metal sheets; and fragmented metal or plastic parts. These are only part of the challenge of using manufactured items that have been changed by accidental means or weathered or worn into their present state.

Experiment with inking and printing procedures and watch for ways to incorporate your "finds" into later prints.

If materials found and brought into the classroom are too dirty, they should be cleaned carefully so the very features that make them interesting are not scraped away. Some surfaces can be steel wooled or steel brushed to clean them up, and yet not destroy the effect they can produce. A careful washing with soapy water will clean up many of the objects brought in, while a simple dusting with a whisk broom will make others more printable.

USING PURPOSELY ALTERED MANUFACTURED OBJECTS

It is possible that occasionally a printmaker can find objects which he wishes to use expressively in his prints. He may purposely use a blowtorch or light a fire on wood or metal to alter its surface; he may pound a strip of metal into a tortuous shape to express the forces of desperation; he may crush a metal container or crack a glass plate or bend or break metal or wood to suit his purpose. The printmaker can score, pound, indent, or otherwise alter the surface of metal, plastic or fiber to suit his own needs.

Such altered materials can provide fascinating and complex textural surfaces which are either esthetically pleasing in themselves or can be incorporated into a relief print composed of several surfaces, shapes, textures and/or colors. Again, experimentation will provide numerous solutions and opportunities to take advantage of such relief surfaces.

Some of these altered materials can be glued, nailed or screwed to boards and become an important part of a designed block.

122

2

5

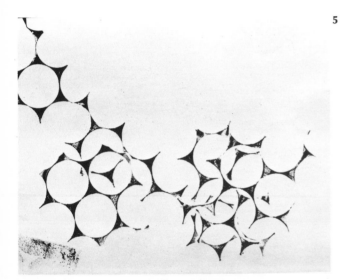

1 *Experimental print made by inking an ordinary piece of gift wrapping ribbon and printing it.*
2 *Four slivers of textured glass, when inked, produced this image.*
3 *A length of masking tape, crumpled and pressed down on a bit of cardboard, makes an interesting printing plate. This one was inked with water soluble ink.*
4 *Two tin cans, one flattened more than the other, provide an interesting experimental study.*
5 *Print made by inking several pieces of the punched metal grill of a furnace filter.*
6 *The crumpled and re-flattened surface of a TV dinner tray produced this textural print. Tempera paint was used instead of printing ink in this effort.*
7 *A flattened frozen food dish, made of soft aluminum, was inked and printed.*

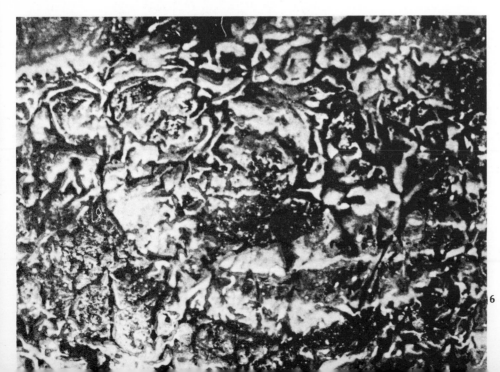

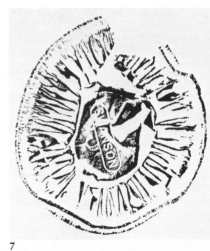

7

6

123

1 *Two flattened tin cans, victims of automobile tires, produce interesting studies when printed.*
2 *Repeat design using a bell pepper and light colored tempera paint, printed on a dark brown surface of construction paper.*
3 *Ever think of printing an ear of Indian corn?*
4 *Leaves and feathers can provide rich learning experiences when the textures and lines are carefully observed. Three prints from Roosevelt High School, Los Angeles.*
5 *Pieces of flattened metal cans, nailed to a board and inked, provide a rich textural print.*
6 *Experimental print made by inking several types of gummed paper labels, without altering their shapes in any way.*

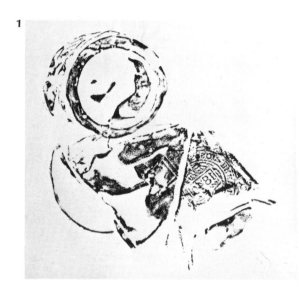

1

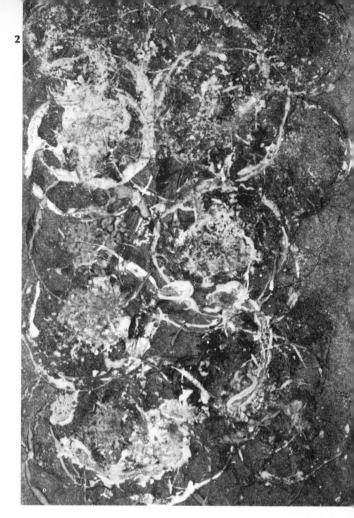

2

3

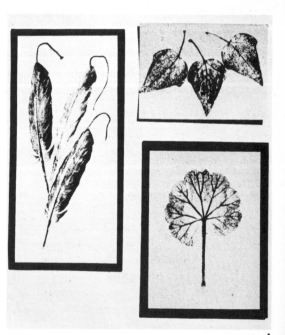

4

Some can be placed in registers and may provide a second color, shape and texture to another print surface. Once their value as printable items is discovered, the challenge might be in finding a place to use them. Or they might simply be enjoyed for their own shapes and surfaces.

PRINTING ORGANIC FORMS

While printing manufactured forms provides the student with an insight into our technological age, pulling images from organic forms will open to him the storehouse of nature-formed shapes. And these shapes, like those pulled from the man-made materials, can be viewed and enjoyed for their own forms, or can be used in conjunction with other materials in more complex prints.

Prints made from fruit and vegetable forms were discussed in chapter 4. Beside these organic shapes, prints can be made from the innumerable leaf forms simply by running an inked (soft or hard) brayer over the leaves, laying a sheet of printing paper over them, and rolling a clean soft rubber brayer over that. The resulting print, if correctly executed, will show the minute and beautiful variations in relief inherent in such natural materials.

Flowers can be pressed between pages of a weighted book or magazine, or between two sheets of weighted blotting paper, and when dry (after several days), can be inked and printed. Leaves can be treated the same way. Care must be taken to ink sparingly, since too much ink will obliterate the fine and subtle relief features.

Experiment with colored inks, papers, printing pressures and techniques.

5

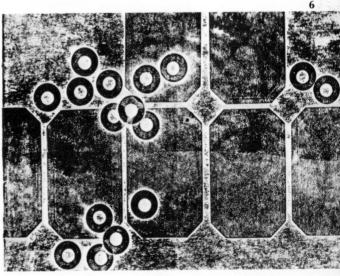

6

GUMMED PAPER THINGS

A visit to a variety or stationery store can bring a few more usable items into the printmaker's repertory of techniques. We, today, manufacture a multitude of things that are gummed or have an adhesive backing. Gather a selection of such materials and see what can be done about building up a surface that will print.

Since the relief features will be very shallow, because the gummed materials are made from paper, a hard rubber brayer should be used to ink the prepared plate. A soft brayer will produce an entirely different effect. Burnishing or pressing will transfer ink to the paper and produce the printed surface.

These items may not be usable in themselves, but remember them when trying to relieve a dull area in a woodcut or linoleum print, because a few gummed labels or stars stuck on the surface of a linoleum block might provide just the surface interest needed.

1

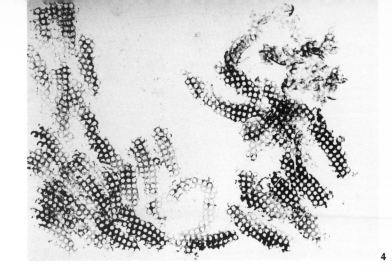

MOVEMENT STUDIES

Marcel Duchamp's studies in painting movement can be used as a point of departure in printing movement. The repetition of the same shape (or slightly altered shape) printed in successively lighter or darker tones will produce a feeling of movement toward the darker tone. This technique can be accomplished by lightening or darkening the ink on successive printings, or it might be done by pressing the same block over and over on the same sheet until the ink is exhausted, moving the block a bit each time away from the first and darkest print.

A rather futuristic and technological feeling is obtained, because of the similarity to the recognizable forms produced by strobo-scopic camera shots, television and motion picture images, and the effects in today's experimental light shows.

Here is a print area that can provide excellent experimental material with ordinary inexpensive materials. Nearly all of the kinds of blocks and surfaces presented in this book may be expanded with the use of this technique.

COLLAGE PRINTING

A variation in the printing technique can provide still another type of result. Build up a collage of various cut and torn papers, with thicker papers providing better relief features. Check the design from time to time, proofing the plate by placing a sheet of news-

1 *A linoleum cut, printed twice with two colors of ink, off register, can produce a study in movement. This surfer, riding a crashing wave, is 24 by 16 in size, and done at Lutheran High School, Los Angeles.*
2 *The brayer need not be rolled to produce a print, this one was just pressed lightly each time to produce a repeating line design.*
3 *The tennis player, reaching to drive a backhand return, is shown in stop action movement. The print (10 x 14) was made from a string print plate, but printed four times, with varying amounts of ink, and definite position-ing each time to produce the feeling of movement. Lutheran High School, Los Angeles.*
4 *An inked golf ball produced this record of its meanderings.*

1

2

3

print over it and rubbing the side of a wax crayon over the back of the paper.

When the design seems complete, follow this interesting variation in printing it: Ink a sheet of linoleum, a block of wood, masonite or sheet of glass the same size as the collage—applying a thin, even layer of ink. On this inked block carefully place a piece of printing paper. Do not ink the collage, but place it face down on the printing paper. (We have the inked uncut block, the printing paper and the face down, uninked collage.) This sandwich can be stood on or run through a press for printing. The raised portions of the collage will produce darker printed areas on the paper, and a soft and delicately patterned print is the result.

If ink surfaces are not the same size as the collage, cut a "frame" out of paper with the opening being the same size as the collage. Lay this frame down over the inked sheet before putting the printing paper down.

Experiment with collage materials, inked surfaces (uncut or cut) and pressing techniques for varied and exciting results.

OTHER PRINTS

Many other surfaces might be tried as printing "plates" once the students feel the value in finding and selecting such materials.

Parts of the body make fascinating prints, revealing delicate and intricate textures that are difficult to duplicate. Try printing the *back* of your hand, your elbow, ankle, knee or nose. All have unique characteristics that are very interesting. Clean-up might be a problem, so it's best to use water soluble paint and have a shower handy.

Pieces of bone can provide shapes and textures, as can a tennis shoe (both the sole and toe), a brayer (try something other than rolling it), and several thousand other items. All can become part of the printmaker's vocabulary.

4

1 *Your elbow has more textures than you might think.*
2 *Try printing the* back *of your hand. The textures might be more interesting than those on your palm.*
3 *A palette knife made these five images. Other knives would add variations to the shapes.*
4 *Nose prints.*

128

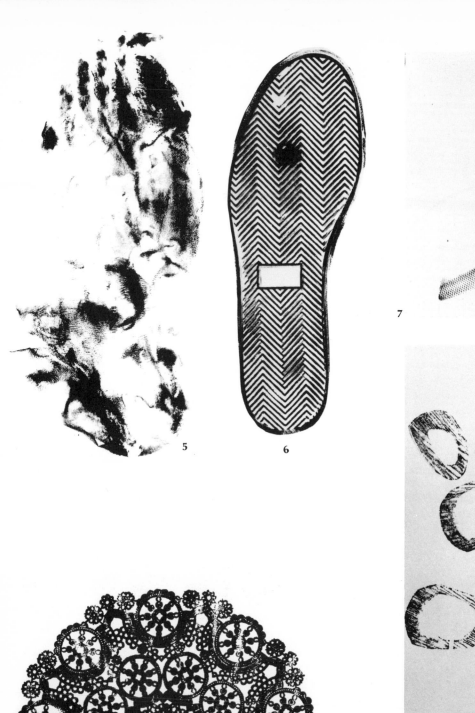

7

9

5 *Print the top of your foot instead of the bottom.*
6 *Print made from the inked sole of a tennis shoe.*
7 *Print made from the toe of a tennis shoe.*
8 *Paper doilies, inked and printed, might be useful in other prints.*
9 *Your dog's teething bone might make an interesting set of prints.*

129

1

2

A FEW MORE IDEAS AND REFERENCES

3

4

Looking back over the previous eight chapters is an awesome experience. Literally dozens of methods of making relief prints are detailed and hundreds are intimated and perhaps more hundreds are left untouched. A compendium of relief print techniques would require volumes—and it would never be completed since new methods are explored nearly every day. We have been given enough, however, to cut our eyeteeth on, and it's up to us and our students to blaze the future trails.

A few disassociated ideas should be presented as a matter of summary and detail, since many of them would have had application in each of the preceding chapters. A discussion on problems and typical assignments is recorded as well as a section dealing with sources for ideas. Also there will be a list of materials that are usable in the various relief printing methods, and some useful references if you are searching for more information.

PROBLEMS AND ASSIGNMENTS

It is difficult to attempt to project a universal assignment into your classroom, because most of the time it will not fit the circumstances, and will fail to inspire your student printmakers to work. However, a few general principles might serve as a guide.

1 *Current problems and student thinking about them are readily transformed into linoleum cut subject matter. Print is 18 by 14, done at Lutheran High School, Los Angeles, California.*
2 *Strength of composition and a yearning to communicate are evident in this 16 by 24 linoleum cut, printed in one color. Los Angeles High School, California.*
3 *Somehow I feel Trapped, in a Bubble. A beautifully flowing design, captured in a tondo composition that is 18 inches in diameter, is a handsome linoleum cut, expressing the student's inner feelings. Los Angeles High School.*
4 *Football. Vigorous action is portrayed in this single color woodcut, 9 x 11½ in size. Interests in sports may lead to new subject matter in many student artists. Lutheran High School, Los Angeles.*

131

1

2

3

Printmaking over the centuries has been spokesman for the desires and aspirations of the masses. When working with wood and linoleum, why not let today's youth speak of their aspirations, gripes, joys and involvements. Motivate with prints of the work of Goya, Grosz and Daumier. Show students the prints and drawings of Munch, Beckman, Posada and Shahn. If involvement and protest are vital to today's young people, let them speak through their prints in as fine a way as they can. There is historical precedent for this outcry, and students can work in this historical context and feel part of the ongoing pattern of the graphic arts.

Involvement can be introduced in broader terms, also. It can deal with student government, world affairs and with urban and rural America. It can be dealt with in terms of religion, sports, nature, government, education and romance. Contemporary and historical events and influences can provide impetus for subject matter. The chance to develop and work in pure design may be challenge enough for some student printmakers.

Studies from sketchbooks, still life set-ups and posed student models might place an emphasis on feeling or design. Portraits, animal studies and areas of music and art can provide exciting ideas and directions of work.

Several of the printmaking techniques lend themselves to working with architectural forms while others might be used to develop concepts of speed, motion, sports, or violent action.

Natural forms might lead to more refined designs. Or abstract designs and forms might be ends in themselves, because of their esthetically pleasing shapes or textures.

When working in the more experimental areas, emphasis should be on the development of surfaces and interest in spatial and linear relationships. Assignments here might involve simply the printing of a number of images with no "picture sense" or design involved, the only goal being the esthetic experience of working with the materials.

Generally speaking, subject matter for problems and assignments should fit the material, and ideas along this line can be gleaned from a glance at the examples in the book. Rather than list specific subjects for problems, the illustrations should suggest ideas that can be adapted to the local, immediate situations.

Since students usually appreciate some restriction or directions to adhere to, they can be made in terms of size (maximum or minimum), use of color (one color or more), materials to be used (wood, linoleum, cardboard, etc.), required number of prints (5 or 10 or so), and so on. Too many restrictions are often stifling, but a few will serve as a guiding directive for the work.

The teacher might indicate a few sample subject matters, or mention that portraits are very effective when working with woodcut. He may indicate that cardboard prints are most useful in developing shape and line concepts in abstract forms. Individual choice of subject, expression and techniques are to be encouraged,

1 *Mythology can provide numerous themes for prints. This 14 by 20 linoleum cut is from Los Angeles High School.*

2 *Varying weights of line provide the interest in this still life linoleum cut. Lutheran High School, Los Angeles.*

3 *Subject matter might also involve rich symbolism, as in this print of the Biblical prophet Isaiah.*

4 *Two-color landscape shows close adherence to the design that was brushed onto the plank with ink. Printed in two shades of brown, the print is 16 by 11½ in size. Lutheran High School, Los Angeles.*

5 *Small blocks of wood might make strong little images. This portrait is only 7 by 6 in size. Lutheran High School, Los Angeles.*

6 *The character of the wood adds strength to portrait studies made from woodcuts. These four are from Lutheran High School, Los Angeles, California, each one being about 15 by 11 in size.*

7 *Put your nose right up to the subject and draw the way it looks. This 18-inch square linoleum cut is of a flute player . . . can you read the fore-shortening? Los Angeles High School.*

8 *Self Portrait. John Knudsen, woodcut, (16 x 16). Portrait studies, done of the artist himself, can provide excellent opportunities for self expression.*

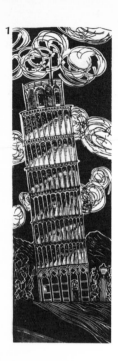

1 Architectural structures can provide excellent material for prints. Both of these are linoleum cuts, the cathedral facade being 16 by 24 in size, and the tower at Pisa being 20 by 7. Both are single color prints. Lutheran High School, Los Angeles.

2 Taos Pueblo. Gerald F. Brommer, woodcut, (11½ x 18). The squarish shapes of the pueblo apartments make a nice contrast to the organic forms of the water carriers.

3 Ornate houses can provide some interesting details for the printmaker. This 20 by 9½ inch woodcut was made on brown paper. Roosevelt High School, Los Angeles.

4 The shape of the wood might determine the subject matter of the print. The vertical feeling of this plank inspired the vertical feeling of a cathedral. Lutheran High School, Los Angeles.

5 Elements in a still life make good subject matter, as in this linoleum cut. Notice the variety of textures the student printmaker was able to use in the 10 by 14 print. Lutheran High School, Los Angeles.

and this might be done in individual consultations as work proceeds.

A class might work together on a large print project, or an individual might want to produce a series of prints. An entire book might be produced, as the Dandelion Book illustrated in chapter 3 or the book depicting Noah's Ark shown at top of pages 136–137.

SOURCES FOR IDEAS

We live in a world that flashes graphic communicative symbols at us constantly, often to the point of distraction, and we should not have to look far for adaptable material for relief printmaking. Magazines abound in photographs that can be worked over for ideas. Find a halftone photo. Make a drawing of it. Eliminate all gray areas, with the lighter grays turned into white and the darker grays into black. Now fill in all the black areas and you have the basis for a relief print.

Trips to museums will prove helpful in developing a feeling of continuity with the printmakers of the past—they all had similar problems. Most museums in our cities have fairly good print collections, while some are outstanding. Several galleries in each city usually specialize in serving print collectors, and often the directors will be happy to spend an afternoon with your students, showing some of their best prints.

Look at natural forms carefully. Weeds, seed pods, flowers, trees, bark, rocks, etc., can provide the beginning of ideas.

A sketching or photographic trip to the zoo might launch a few new ideas, or so might a trip around the city in a school bus, or recollections from a summer in Europe or a trip to the mountains, desert, or seashore.

School Arts magazine is filled with ideas that are either directly related to printmaking or can provide avenues of association for other ideas.

If you are interested in more books that offer ideas or techniques, the following are among the best available:

ARTISTS PROOF, VOLUME VII
Published by the Pratt Center for Contemporary Printmaking, New York. Some excellent examples of contemporary printmaking techniques.

PRINTS FROM LINOBLOCKS AND WOODCUTS
Manly Banister; Sterling Publishing Co., Inc., New York, 1967. Complete coverage of techniques, materials and tools from idea to matted print.

GRAPHIC DESIGN: A CREATIVE APPROACH
Matthew Baranski; International Textbook Co., Scranton, Pennsylvania, 1960. Presents a wide variety of graphic processes for all grade levels; shows and describes student work.

A HANDBOOK OF GRAPHIC REPRODUCTION PROCESSES
Felix Brunner, Hastings House, New York, 1968. A complete outline of all printmaking processes.

4

5

1

2

3

PRINTMAKING WITHOUT A PRESS
Jane D. Erickson and Adelaide Sproul; Van Nostrand Reinhold, New York, 1966. Concise and informative with a good selection of prints.

PRINTMAKING WITH A SPOON
Norman Gorbaty; Reinhold Publishing Corp., New York, 1960. Emphasis on various aspects of relief printing without a press.

SURFACE PRINTING
Peter Green; Watson-Guptill, New York, 1968. How to make relief prints from almost any raised surface around us.

PRINTMAKING TODAY
Jules Heller; Henry Holt and Co., New York, 1958. Extremely fine coverage of all printmaking techniques, with emphasis on the classic approaches. Very complete in every respect.

YOUNG PRINTMAKERS, II (Portfolio)
Edited by F. Louis Hoover, Davis Publications, Worcester, Massachusetts, 1969. Excellent examples of student work with student-artists' comments.

ESKIMO PRINTS
James Houston, Barre Publishers, Barre, Massachusetts, 1967. A wonderfully exciting volume dealing primarily with relief stone cuts that excel in simplicity and strength of design.

NANTUCKET WOODCUTS
Naoko Matsubara and Fritz Eichenberg; Barre Publishers, Barre, Massachusetts, 1967. Dynamic illustrations in woodcut by Naoko Matsubara that are stimulating examples of the printmaker's craft.

THE MODERN JAPANESE PRINT: AN APPRECIATION
James A. Michener; Tuttle, Rutland, Vermont. Analyzes ten tipped-on reproductions and discusses those and other contemporary and experimental printmaking techniques.

PRINTMAKING ACTIVITIES FOR THE CLASSROOM
Arnel Pattemore; Davis Publications, Worcester, Massachusetts, revised and enlarged 1969. Very fine coverage of many techniques both traditional and experimental.

PRINTMAKING (Printmaking Methods Old and New)
Gabor Perterdi; the Macmillan Co., New York, 1959. A fine discussion of the traditional and contemporary approaches to all phases of printmaking. Excellent section on the woodcut.

FRONTIERS OF PRINTMAKING
Michael Rothenstein; Reinhold Publishing Corp., New York, 1966. Stimulating result of research in experimental relief printing.

7

5

6

LINOCUTS AND WOODCUTS
Michael Rothenstein; Watson-Guptill Publ., New York, 1962. Complete discussion on the traditional and contemporary handling of relief techniques.

EXPERIMENTS IN RELIEF PRINTMAKING
Charles Smith; University of Virginia Press, 1954. Emphasis on the experimental approaches to the relief print.

PRINTMAKING, HISTORY AND TECHNIQUE
Kristian Sotriffer; McGraw-Hill Book Co., New York, 1968. Fine historical and technical account of every major printmaking technique.

1 *This woodcut camel makes fine use of the variety of textures available to the conventional student printmaker.*
2 *Bird forms can be suggested by printmaking as readily as in any other medium. These egrets are done in woodcut, 24 by 9 in size. Lutheran High School, Los Angeles.*
3 *Nebraska. David Kohl, woodcut, (18 x 11¹/₂). A single boot can be expressive of a whole way of life.*
4 *The organic forms of trees, flowers or thistles might be fascinating to some young printmakers. Both of these are woodcuts and come from Lutheran High School, Los Angeles.*
5 *Student interest in musical groups might lead to print subject matter. These four musicians, done in 20 by 16 linoleum are from Lutheran High School, Los Angeles.*
6 *A complicated still life can provide a real challenge to the printmaker. This woodcut (11¹/₂ x 24) is done in two colors. Lutheran High School, Los Angeles.*
7 *Book projects might be worked on by the entire class, although this one of Noah's Ark was done by Arthur Geisert. Each page is same size and folds out to long frieze.*

137

1 *Thin strips of scrap wood might be put to excellent use, as this 12 by 3½ inch print shows. Roosevelt High School, Los Angeles.*

2 *With Something Above and Something Below. Richard Wiegmann, woodcut, (12 x 18). Full figures and groups of figures in action or standing arrangements can provide innumerable compositions.*

3 *Walking Couple is a woodcut, 10 by 6 in size. Lutheran High School, Los Angeles.*

4 *The Box. Lee Hanson, woodcut, (23 x 17). This large woodcut, done in two colors on white paper, shows a vibrating quality due to the technique used in carving on the background for the figure. Notice the stylization of the muscle structure in the crouched figure. Courtesy, Orlando Gallery, Encino, California.*

5 *Some students might like working in fine detail, and linoleum cuts may provide an outlet for them. This African village, with its fine lines, is only 8 by 6 in size. Lutheran High School, Los Angeles.*

6 *Subject matter might be found in simplification of complex subject matter, as in this linoleum cut done from a painting. Luther High School North, Chicago.*

PRINTMAKING: A MEDIUM FOR BASIC DESIGN
Peter Weaver; Reinhold Publishing Corp., New York, 1968. Emphasis on experimental techniques and application of techniques to design problems.

GREAT PRINTS AND PRINTMAKERS
Herman F. Wechsler, Harry N. Abrams, Inc., New York, 1967. Examples of the major printmaking techniques illustrated with master prints by the world's all-time leaders in each field.

INTRODUCING WOODCUTS
Gerald Woods; Watson Guptill, New York, 1969. Emphasis on woodcut, but other contemporary relief methods are also covered.

PRINTS AND HOW TO MAKE THEM
Arthur Zaidenberg; Harper and Row, New York, 1964. Major printmaking techniques discussed fully, with excellent illustrations.

Paper Covered Books

HOW TO DO LINOLEUM BLOCK PRINTING
Mary E. Hicks; Foster Art Service, Inc., Tustin, California. Complete directions for working with linoleum, with emphasis on the multi-color prints.

PRINTMAKING
Dona Z. Meilach; Pitman Publishing Corp., New York, 1965. Concise explanations of the major areas of printmaking.

WOODCUT
Harry Sternberg; Pitman Publishing Corp., New York, 1962. Fine explanation of the techniques for working the woodcut, especially the multicolor print and some experimental techniques.

WATER SOLUBLE OIL

A product referred to from time to time in the book is a water soluble oil which is the development of the Weber Costello Company of Chicago. Obtainable under the trade name of Printoleum, it is a brownish transparent material of thin honey-like consistency. It can be mixed on the ink slab with powdered tempera or dry pigments to get any color, tint or shade required. Mixed with a palette knife and applied to the block with a brayer, everything can be cleaned up with water. But the consistency of the ink and resulting properties of the ink and the print are similar to oil printing ink which must be cleaned with turpentine or paint thinner.

A SAVING ON INK

Some teachers have found from experience, that the ink slabs need not be cleaned after every period. When successive periods will use the plates (or even left overnight), they can be successfully rerolled with fresh ink added at the edge of the slab. A noticeable

5

6

139

1

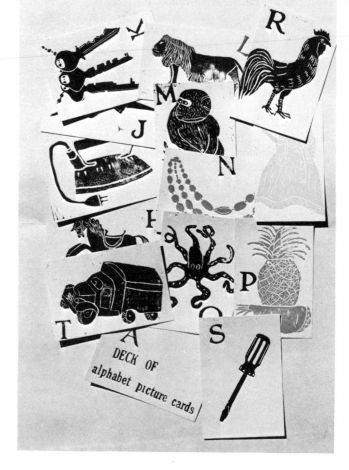

2

3

4

5

saving of ink can be achieved in this way. Brayers should still be cleaned after each period of use, unless the next class will pick up where the earlier one left off.

NUMBERING AND SIGNING THE PRINT

When the set of printed images is dry, the prints should be trimmed so about two inches of clean paper form a border around the print. At the lower left corner of the print, and directly *under* it should be penciled the title of the print if it has one. Directly *under* the center of the print should be the numbering of each copy. This number should appear as a fraction. For example, 3/10 means that there were ten copies of the print of which this is number three. The top number indicates the number of this print, the lower figure the number of prints in the edition. Directly *under* the print in the lower right-hand corner should be placed the signature of the printmaker. All of this information is correctly recorded in pencil.

It is a good idea for student printmakers to conclude their activity with this signing ritual, since the print is only then completed.

MATTING THE PRINT

If matting the print is required it can be done in several ways but the accepted method is done with a hinged mat. The opening in the mat should be larger than the edge of the printed surface: about 1/4 inch larger at the top and sides and 1/2 inch larger at the bottom to accommodate the numbering and signature that is directly under the print. A two- or three-inch mat is usually used. A backing board (chipboard or other cardboard) is cut the same size as the front mat board, and these are hinged together with paper tape along the top edge. The print itself is tipped (pasted) or taped by the edges to the backing board, positioned to fit in the cut opening of the front mat.

MATERIALS

Many materials are listed in various parts of the book, most of them being interchangeable with the various processes. Here is a consolidated list of materials arranged in various categories. Not all of them are required for printmaking classes, however, and the list merely shows what can be used if available.

1 A calendar might provide material for a group project. The letters and numbers in this one are silk screened while the illustration is a linoleum cut. Bancroft Junior High School, Los Angeles.
2 A deck of alphabet picture cards was a class project involving linoleum cuts. This colorful set comes from Bancroft Junior High School, Los Angeles.
3 The printmaker should sign his name in pencil below the lower right-hand corner of the print.
4 The print should be tipped or taped to the backing board, and the mat should be hinged at the top edge of the board.
5 The hinged mat then falls in place over the print, allowing a small margin of paper to appear around the print, especially at the bottom where the title, number and signature of the artist appear.

PAPER FOR PRINTING
Newsprint (for proofing)
Bond paper
Oatmeal paper
Bogus paper
Construction paper
Drawing paper
Rice papers of various types
3M Printmakers Fabric
Tableau Block Printing Paper
Speedball Printmasters Block Printing Paper
Mulberry paper
Pelon, medium or heavyweight (waxless)

TOOLS FOR CUTTING THE BLOCKS
Stanley knife
Mat knife
X-acto knife set, with various blades
U-shaped gouges
V-shaped veiners
Chisels
Linozip pull cutters
Spoon gouge

TOOLS FOR MARKING THE BLOCKS
Hammer
Screwdriver and chisel
Nails and screws of different sizes
Wires of various types
Rasps and files
Staples and staple guns
Knives
Punches
Ice Pick

SHARPENING STONES FOR CUTTING TOOLS
Axolite stone
Indian carborundum oil stone
Washita stone
Arkansas stone
Slip stones for sharpening the inside of gouges and veiners
Oil can for the stones

ELECTRIC TOOLS FOR USE ON BLOCKS
Drills and bits
Wire brush attachment
Sander
Circular saw
Router
Saber saw

BURNISHERS
Wooden spoon
Tablespoon or soup spoon
Baren
Smooth bottom of bottle
Smooth flat stone
Bone or metal burnishers
Rice paddle (wood)

WOOD FOR WOODCUTS (PLANKWOOD)
White pine
Yellow pine
Parana pine
Pear
Cherry
Beech
Sycamore
Plywoods
Masonite

INKS
Water soluble ink
Oil based ink
Printoleum
Oil paint
Printers ink
Tempera (for certain prints)

GLUES
Polyvinyl acetate
  Elmer's Permagrip
  Borden's
  Wilhold
Duco cement
Airplane glue
Rubber cement

LIQUIDS THAT TURN TO SOLIDS
Sculpmetal
Liquid Steel
Liquid Aluminum
Gesso
P.V.A. glues
Casting resins
Cement

TOOLS FOR CUTTING CARDBOARDS AND PAPER
Scissors
Paper cutter
Single edge razor blades
X-acto knives
Mat knife
Stanley knife

CARDBOARD AND PAPER FOR SURFACE INTEREST OR FOR BLOCK MAKING
Tissue paper
Construction paper
Corrugated cardboard
Chipboards
Tagboards
Railroad boards
Poster board
Mat board
Folio board

BRAYERS
Solid soft rubber roller
Solid hard rubber roller
Wood core hard rubber roller
Gelatin roller

FOR TEXTURING WOOD OR BUILDING UP RELIEF
Nails, staples
Pins, washers
Sand, gravel
Glues, gesso
Modeling paste
String, cord
Gears, machine parts
Nuts and bolts
Screen, hardware cloth
Textiles, scraps of cloth
Watch and clock parts
Sheet metal, tin cans
Aluminum sheeting
Metal foil, mesh
Copper sheet
Used offset photo plates
Toothpicks
Applicator sticks

1 The printroom rack on which this multitude of experiments are drying, can become a most interesting viewing area.
2 Plywood panels provide excellent surfaces from which to print wood grains.
3 A single image of Mark Twain, printed three times, producing a large 14 x 24 woodcut image. Lutheran High School, Los Angeles.
4 Football player of paper, string, cardboard and glue is charging through more glue. Collagraph is 18 by 12 and inked with umber oil paint. Lutheran High School, Los Angeles.

HISTORICAL INFORMATION

The woodcuts and relief prints of many fine artists have been reproduced for study in books and as individual prints. Among the lengthy list of historically important relief printmakers whose work can help shape the direction of student activity are the following:

Leonard Baskin
Hans Beckman
Thomas Bewick
George Braque
Gustave Dore
Jean Dubuffet
Roul Dufy
Albrecht Dürer
Lyonel Feininger
Antonio Frasconi
Paul Gauguin
Haronobu
Stanley W. Hayter
Hiroshige
Katsushika Hokusai
Hans Holbein

Wassily Kandinsky
Ernst Ludwig Kirchner
Misch Kohn
Kathe Kollwitz
Henri Matisse
Joan Miro
Shiko Munakata
Emil Nolde
Pablo Picasso
Jose Guadalupe Posada
Rudy Pozzatti
Michael Rothenstein
Karl Schmidt-Rottluff
Kurt Schwitters
Harry Sternberg
Maurice Vlaminck

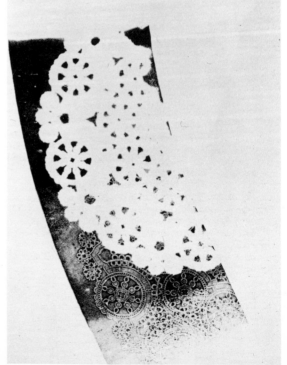

2

1

3

Other printmakers, not specialists in relief printing but working in other media, whose work might lead students into various directions:

Ernst Barlach
Lee Chesney
Honore Daumier
Stuart Davis
Edgar Degas
Francisco Goya
William Hogarth

James McNeill Whistler
Jose Clemente Orozco
Rembrandt van Rijn
George Rouault
Ben Shahn
Martin Schongauer
Henri de Toulouse-Lautrec

Books which deal with the history of printmaking can help provide impetus to some students. Most books on printmaking seem to carry some reference material, but some are more complete than others. Any of these might be placed in the classroom for reference, or can be referred to in the library for further study.

A HISTORY OF WOOD ENGRAVING
D. P. Bliss; J. M. Dent and Sons, Ltd., London, 1928.

PRINTMAKING TODAY
Jules Heller; Henry Holt and Co., New York, 1960.

THE FLOATING WORLD
James Michener; Random House, New York, 1954.

MODERN PRINTS AND DRAWINGS
Paul J. Sachs; Alfred A. Knopf, New York, 1954.

500 YEARS OF ART IN ILLUSTRATION
Howard Simon; Garden City Publishing Co., Inc., Garden City, New York, 1949.

SHIKO MUNAKATA
Yoyuro Yasada; Charles E. Tuttle Co., Vermont, 1958.

THE EXPRESSIONISTS
Carl Zigrosser; Thames and Hudson, London, 1957.

4

1 *Untitled letterhead: ships. Lyonel E. Feininger, woodcut on yellow paper, (3¹/₈ x 4³/₈ block size). The artist produced many of his own letterheads which would accompany the notes he would write. Collection, Pasadena Art Museum, California. Bequest, Galka E. Scheyer Estate.*
2 *Vivace. Richard Wiegmann, woodcut and serigraph, (21 x 15). An exuberant statement that successfully combines two mediums of the printmakers' art. Combinations of other printmaking techniques might be easily explored. Collection of the author.*
3 *A brayer, rolled across the raised form of the paper doily, prints it as a negative shape, but repeats all the doily's intricacies when the rolling continues.*
4 *Lecture Notes. Arthur Thall, intaglio, (22³/₄ x 18). The use of letters can lead to some interesting graphic arrangements. Courtesy, Orlando Gallery, Encino, California.*

ACKNOWLEDGEMENTS

One of the wonderful things about working on a book like this is the opportunity to meet and work with a great number of knowledgeable and cooperative people—many of them experts in their fields. For their unstinting help, which often far exceeded the requests, I would like to express my thanks to the following: Fred Parker, Curator of Prints, Pasadena Art Museum, Pasadena, California; Mrs. M. M. Shinno, who represents many contemporary Japanese printmakers; Ruth M. Ebken, Associate Director of Art Instruction for the Pittsburgh Public Schools; Betsy Gilchrist at Bancroft Junior High School, Los Angeles, California; Helen Luitjens at Revere Junior High School, Los Angeles; Stuart Allingham at Los Angeles High School, Los Angeles; Lois McMillan at Roosevelt and Eagle Rock High Schools, Los Angeles; Don Williams and Al Porter, Secondary Art Supervisors for the Los Angeles City Schools; David Kohl at Luther High School North, Chicago, Ill.; Roland Sylwester at Lutheran High School, Los Angeles; Joseph E. Young and Ebria Feinblatt, Curator of Prints and Drawings at the Los Angeles County Museum of Art; Richard Tooke, Supervisor of Rights and Reproductions at the Museum of Modern Art in New York; Richard Wiegmann at Concordia Teachers College, Seward, Nebraska; Anita Ribas of London Arts Incorporated, Detroit, Michigan; Virginia Timmons, of the Division of Art Education in the Baltimore City Public Schools, Maryland; Arthur Geisert at Concordia Teachers College in River Forest, Illinois; and to the many others who offered help and suggestions. Special thanks to George Horn who kept the pressure on; to Helen Dahl, Becky Littmann and Laura Steinweg who printed and printed and printed; and to my wife, Georgia, who doled out unmeasurable encouragement.

GFB

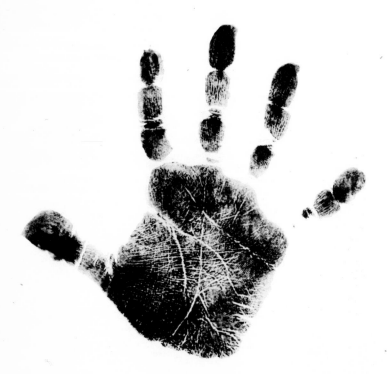

148